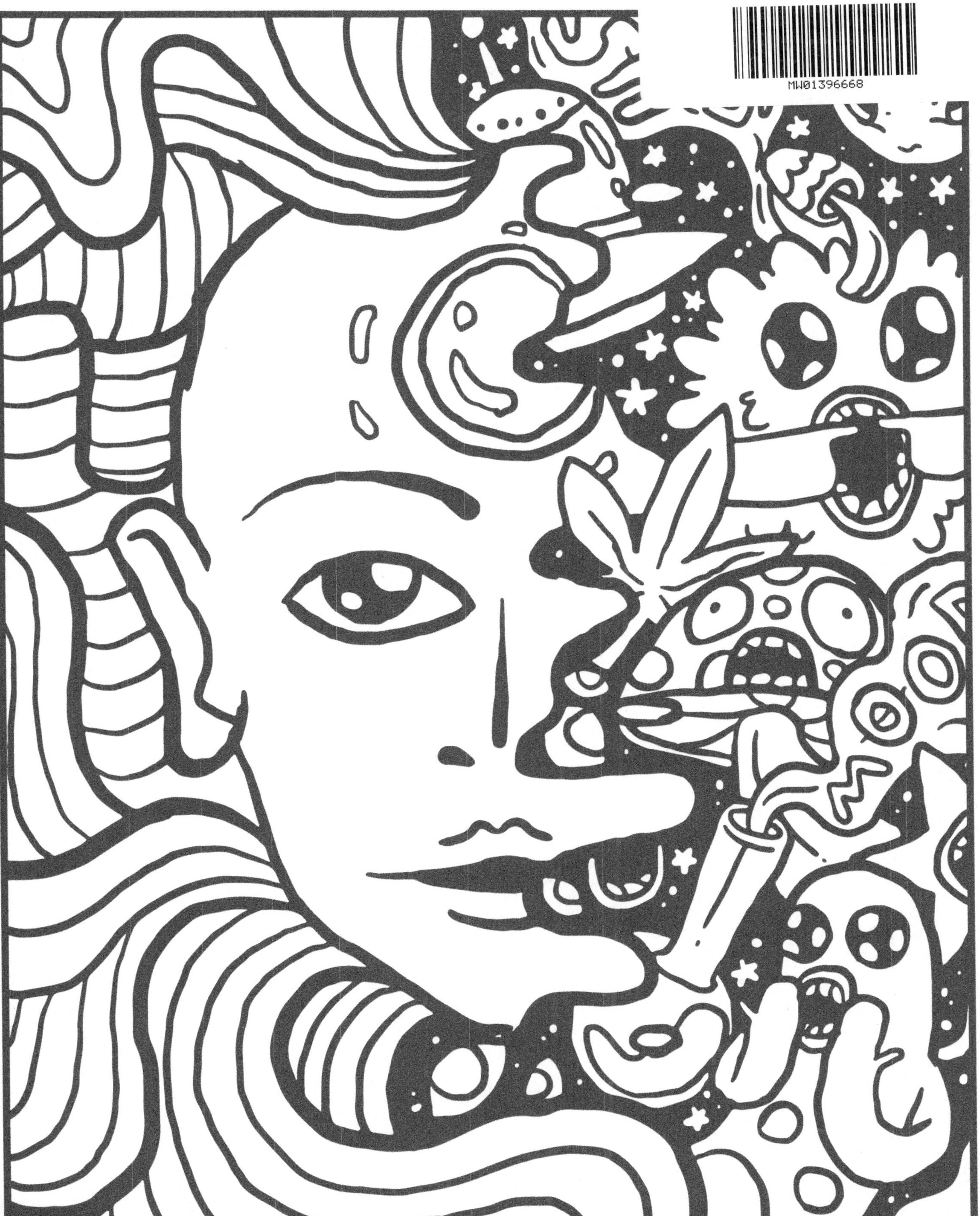

MW01396668

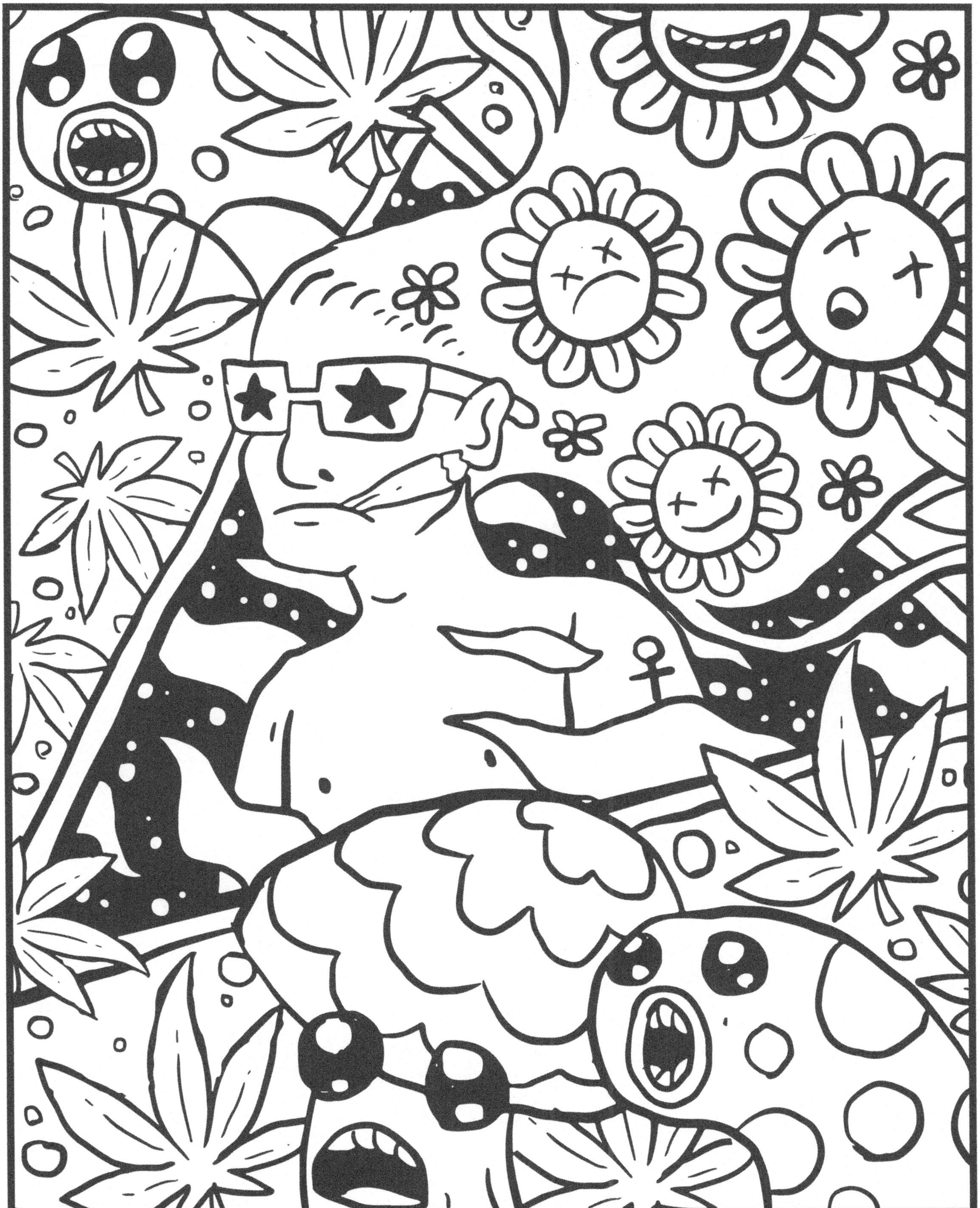

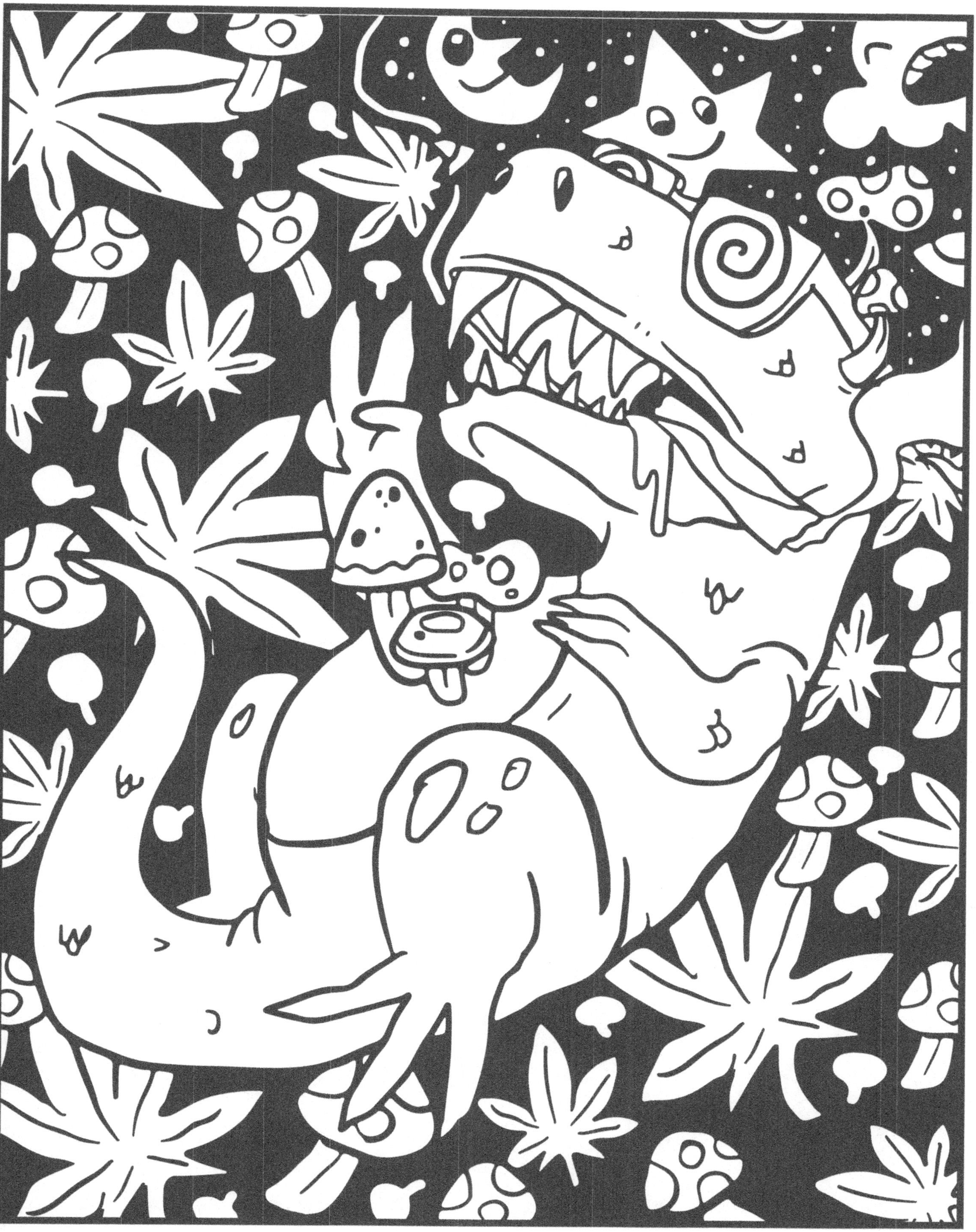

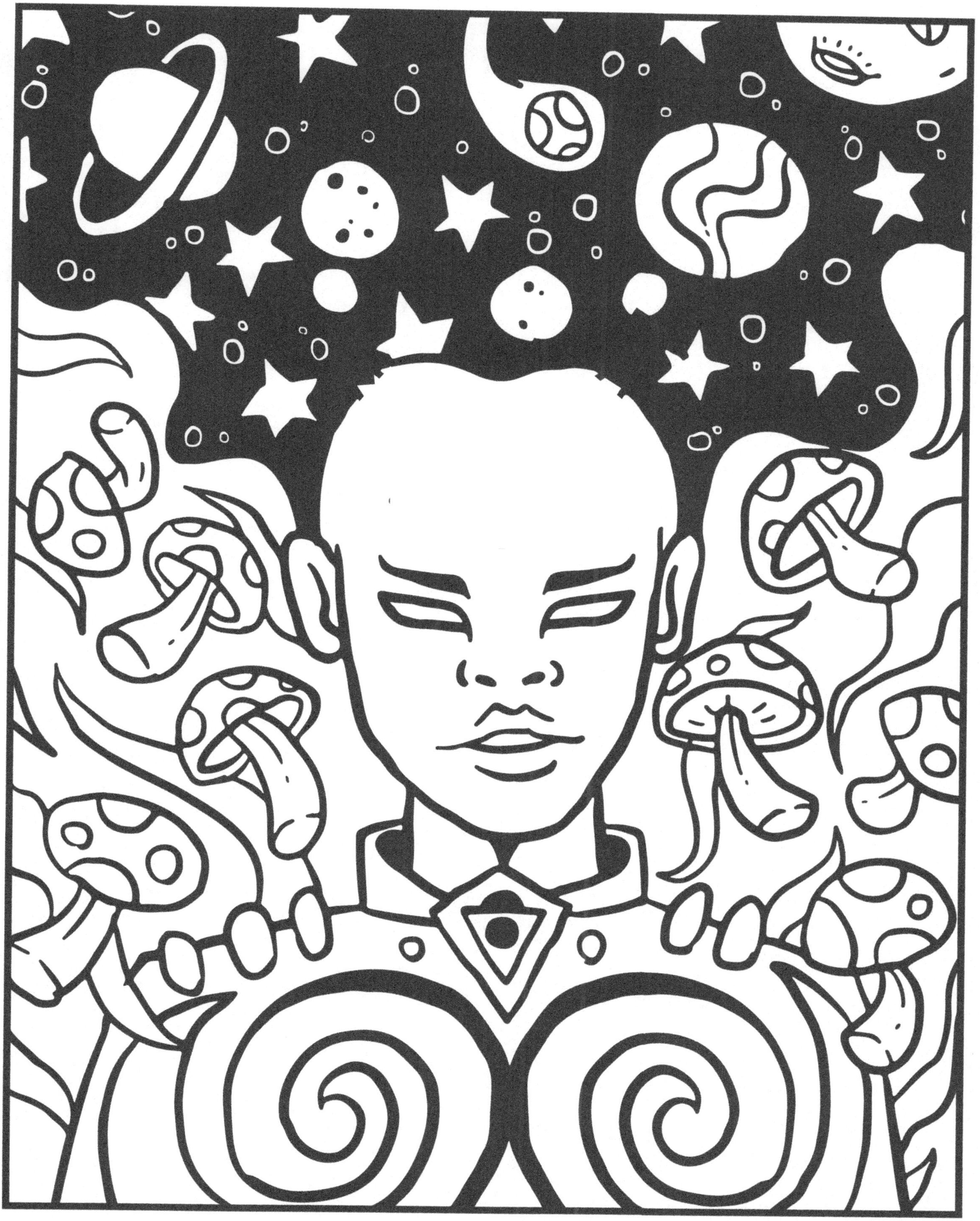

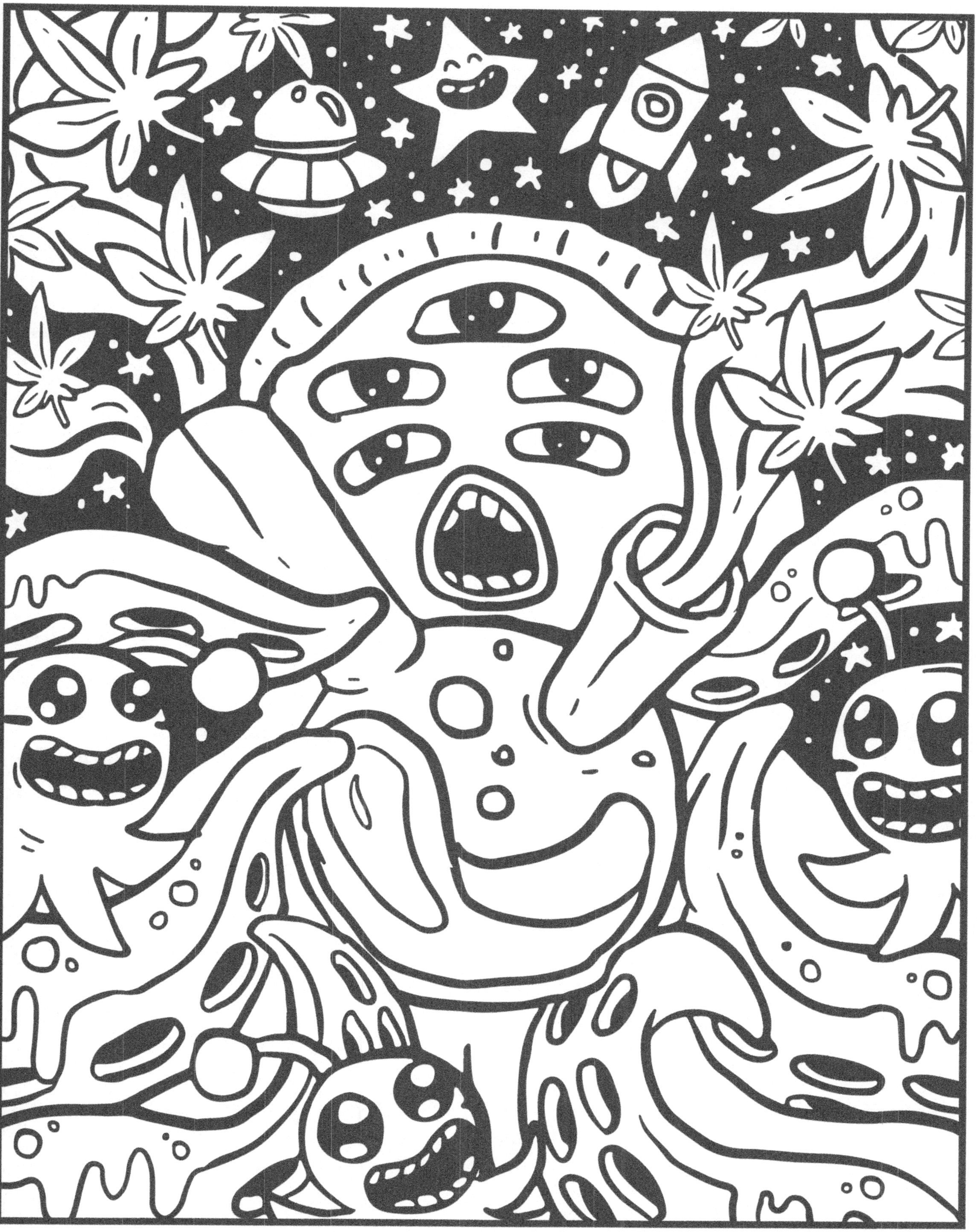

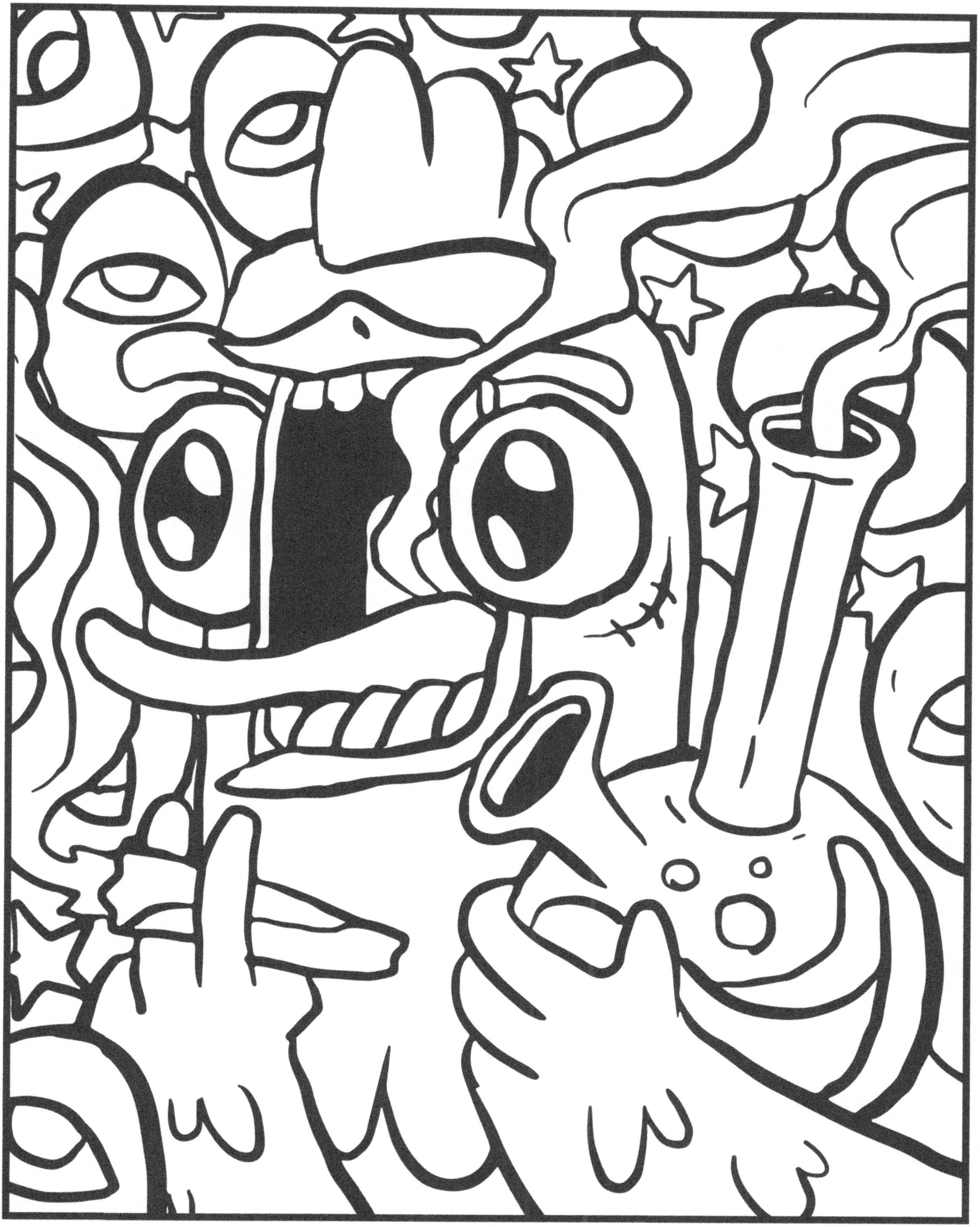

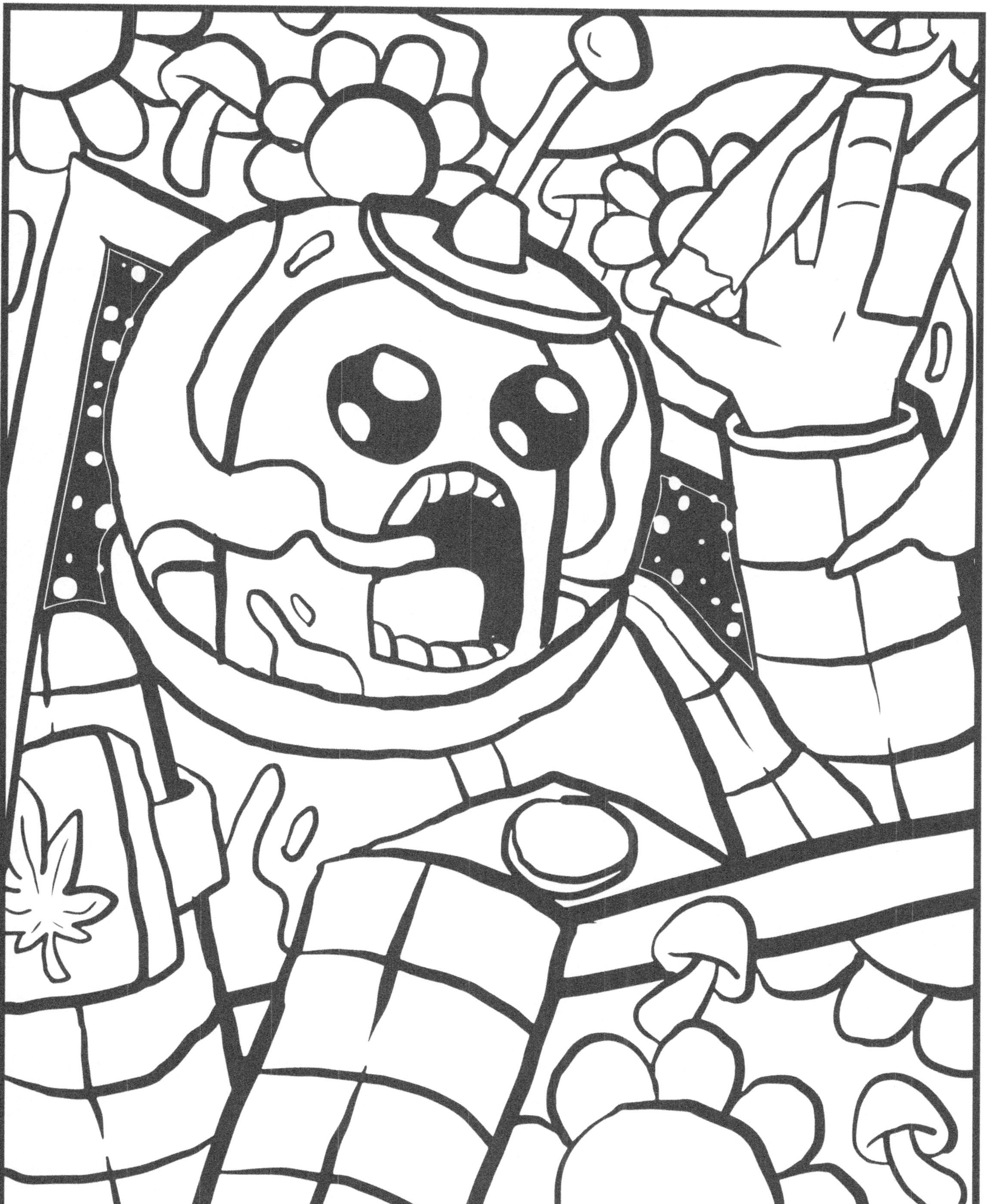

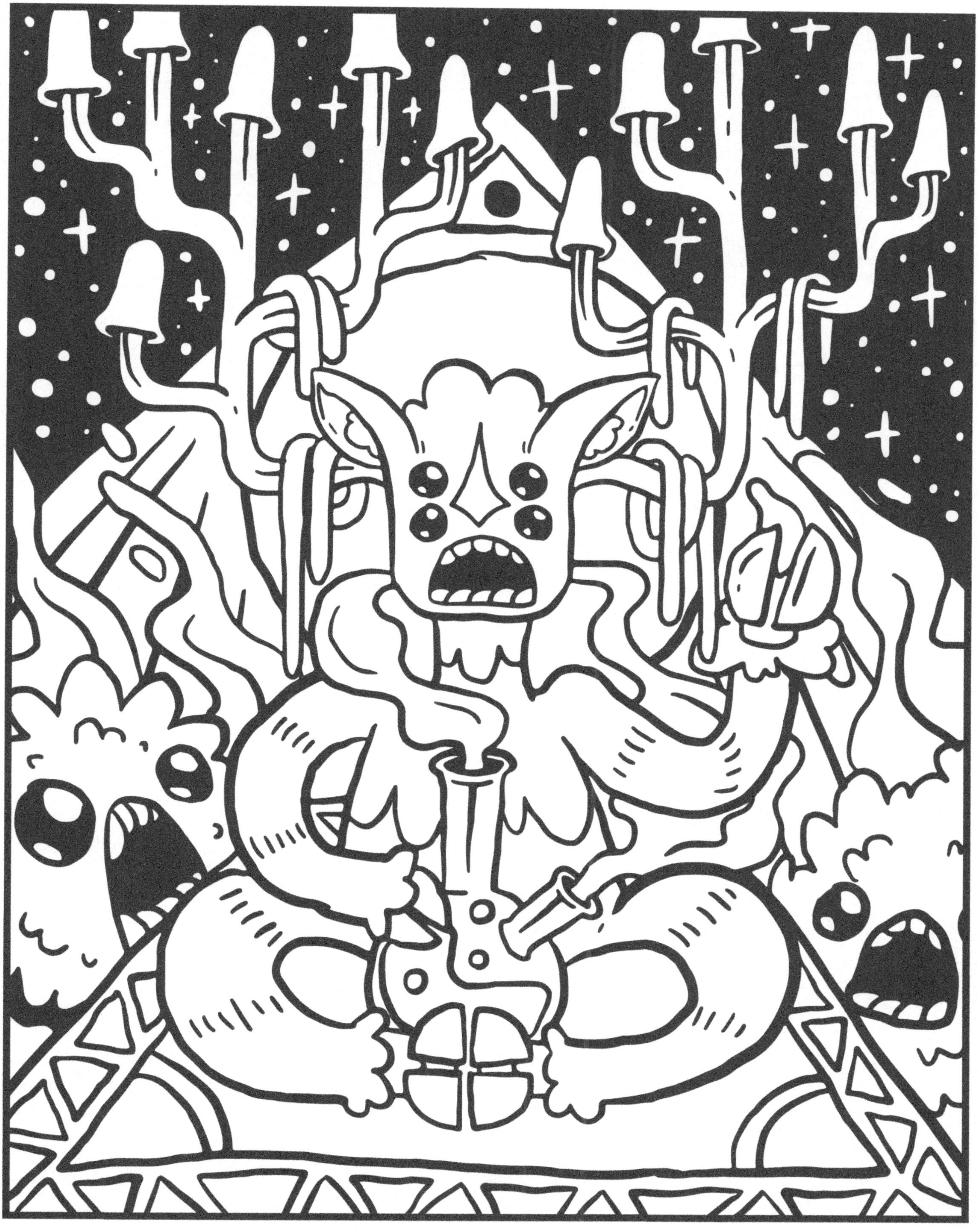

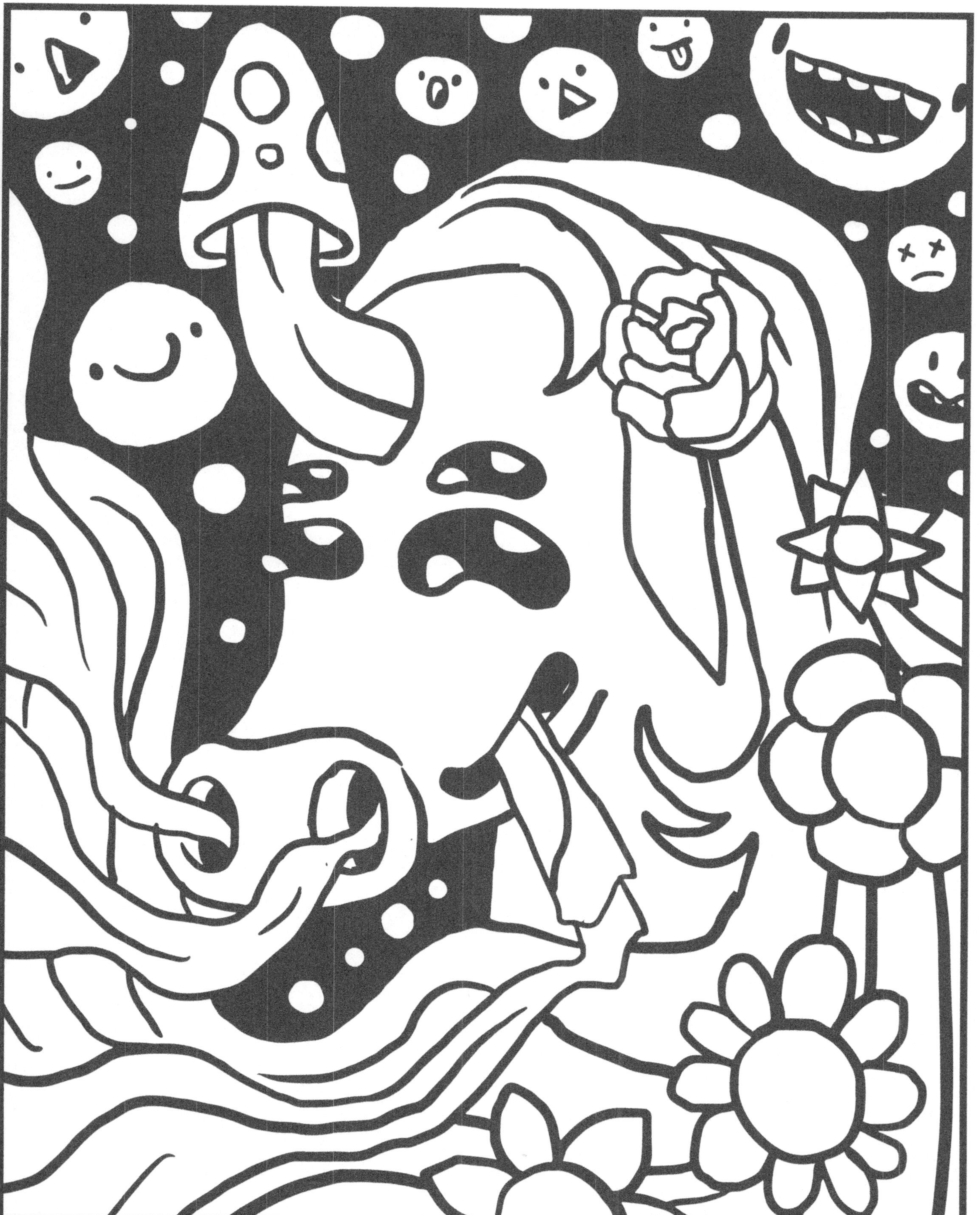

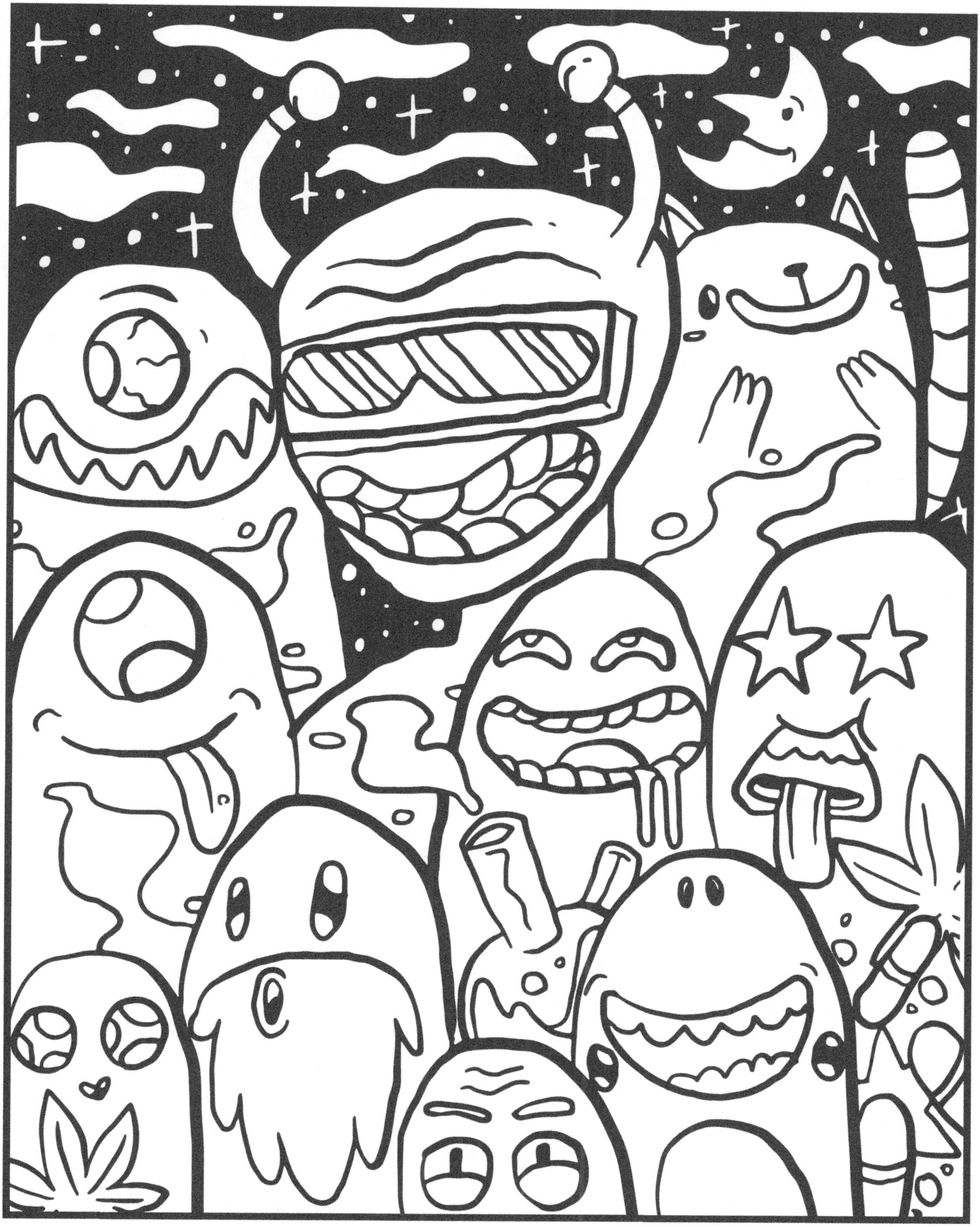

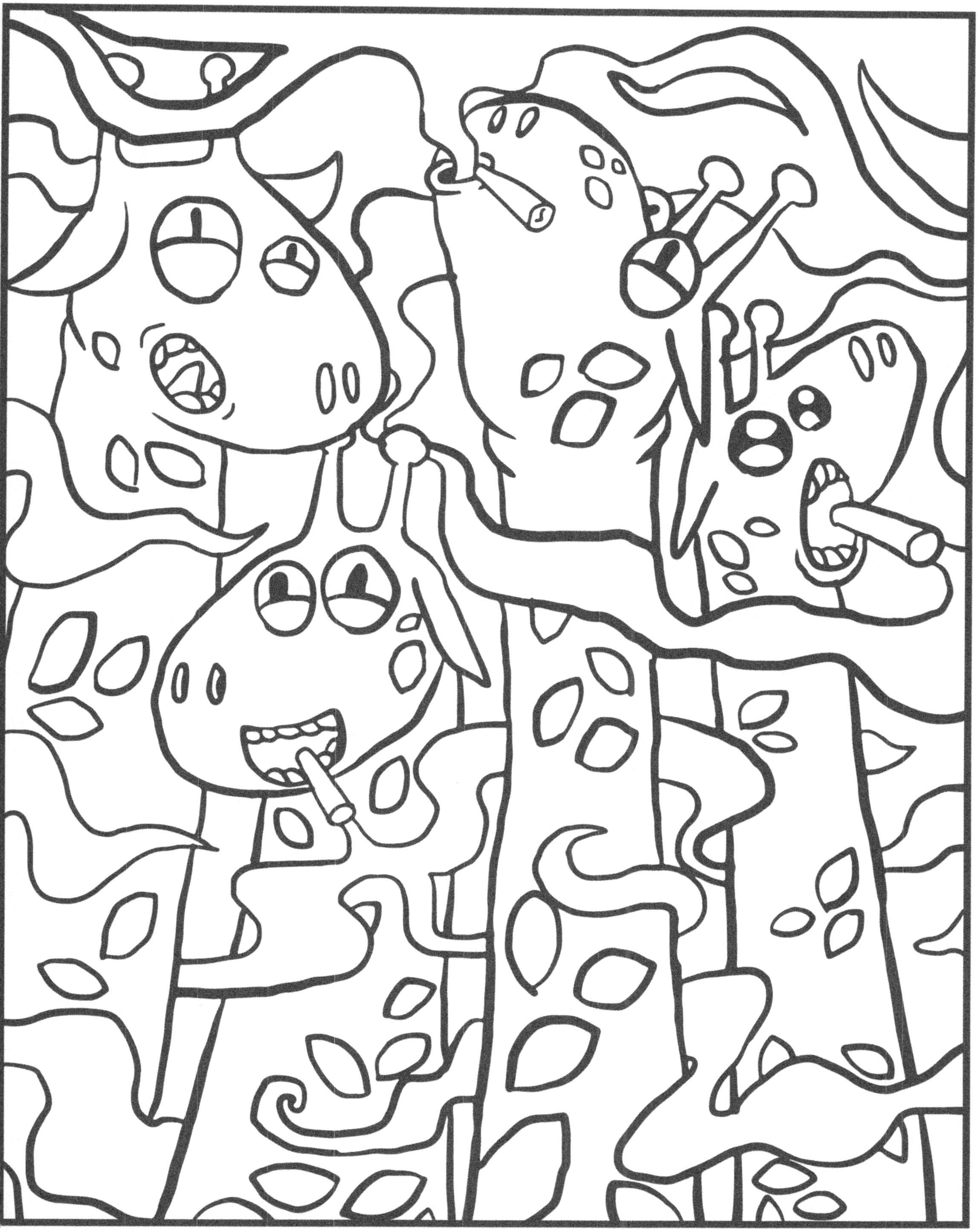

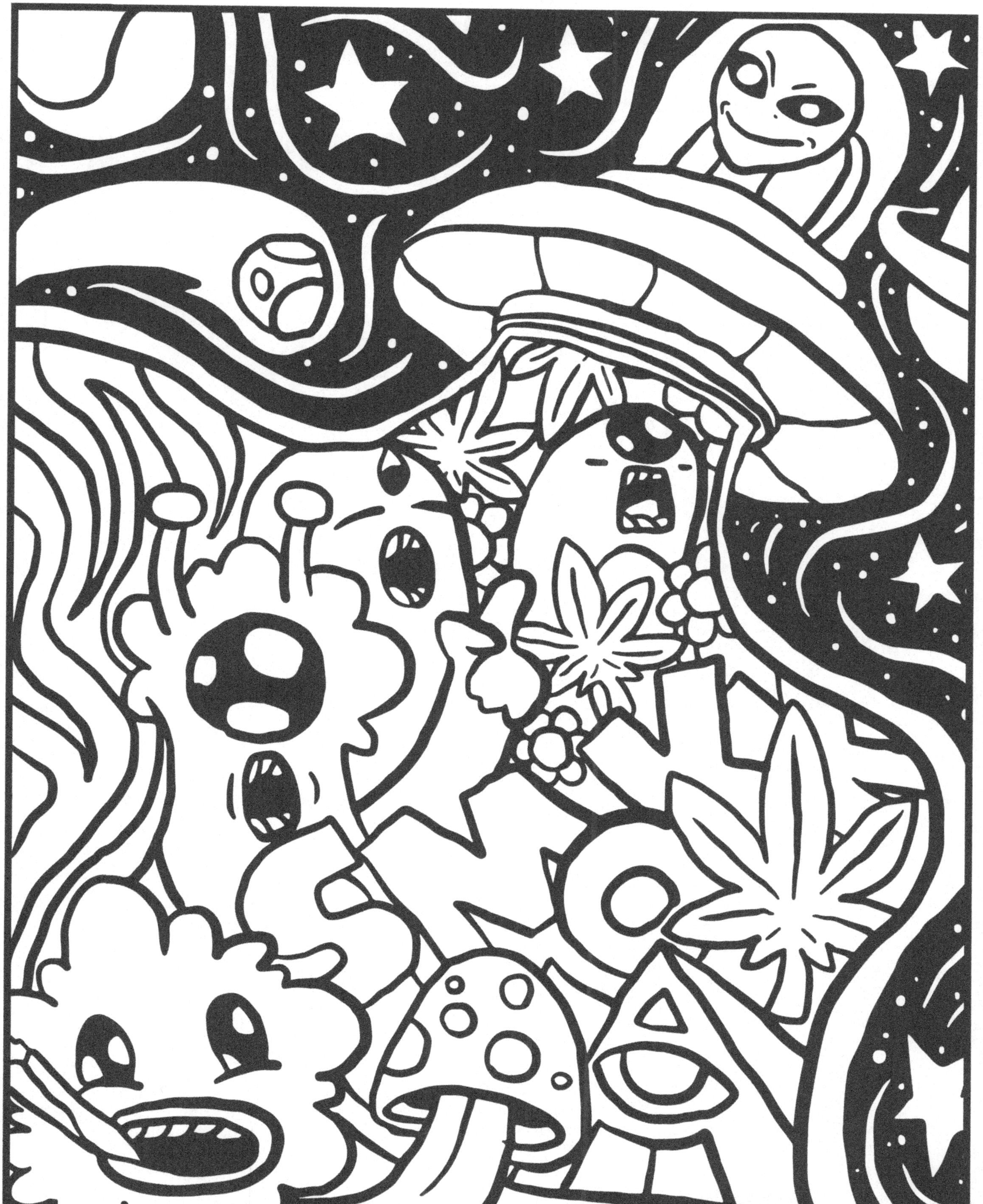

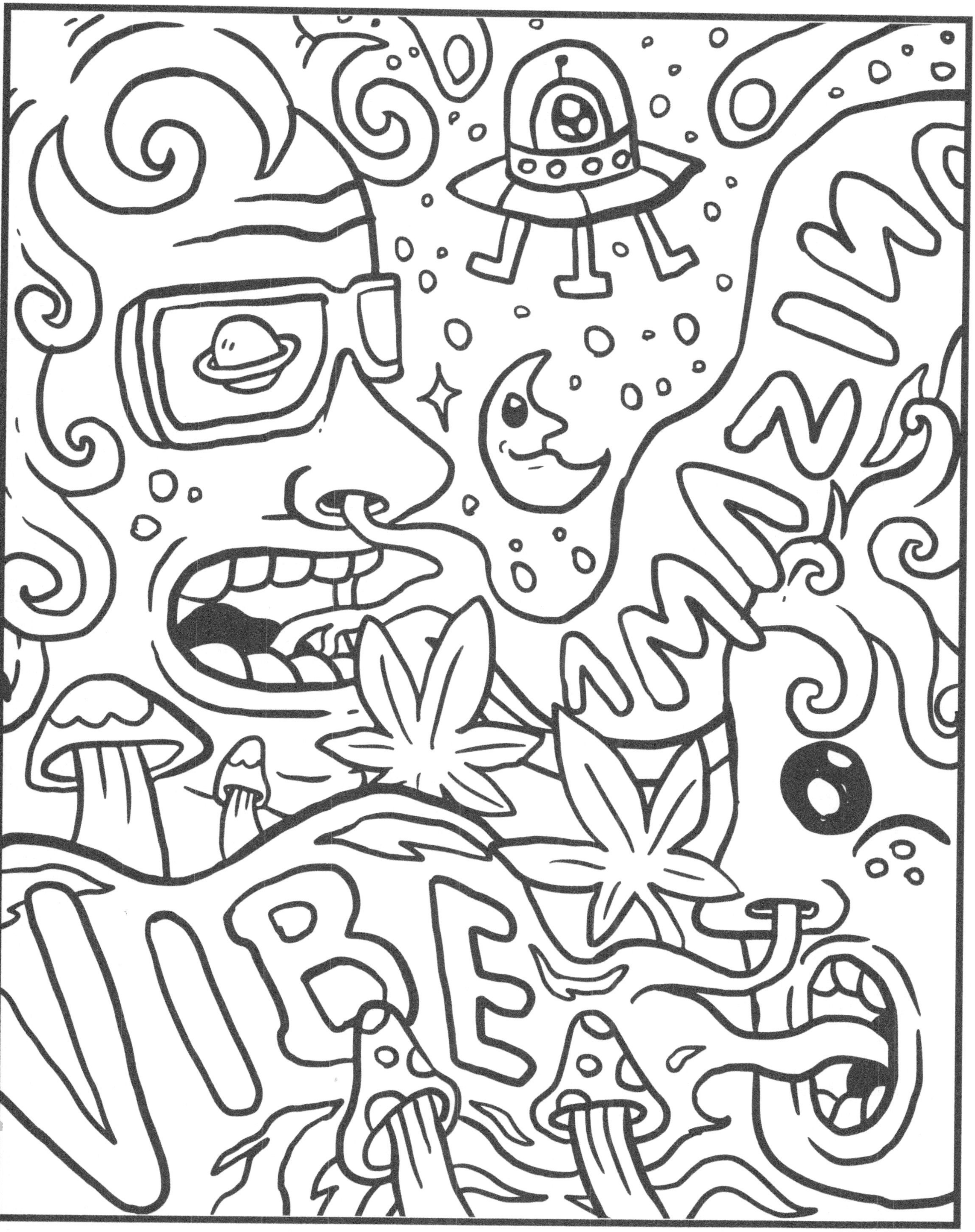

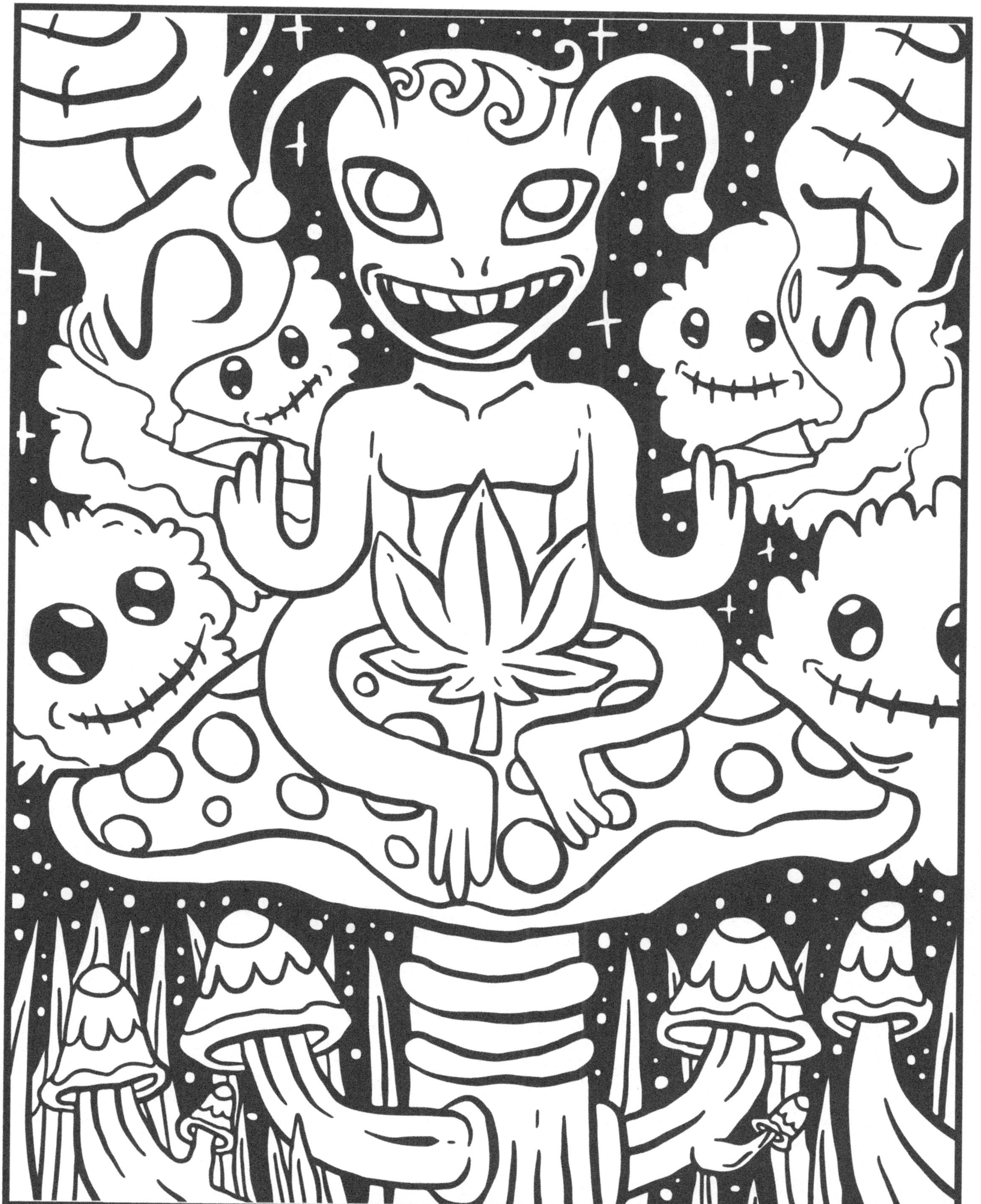

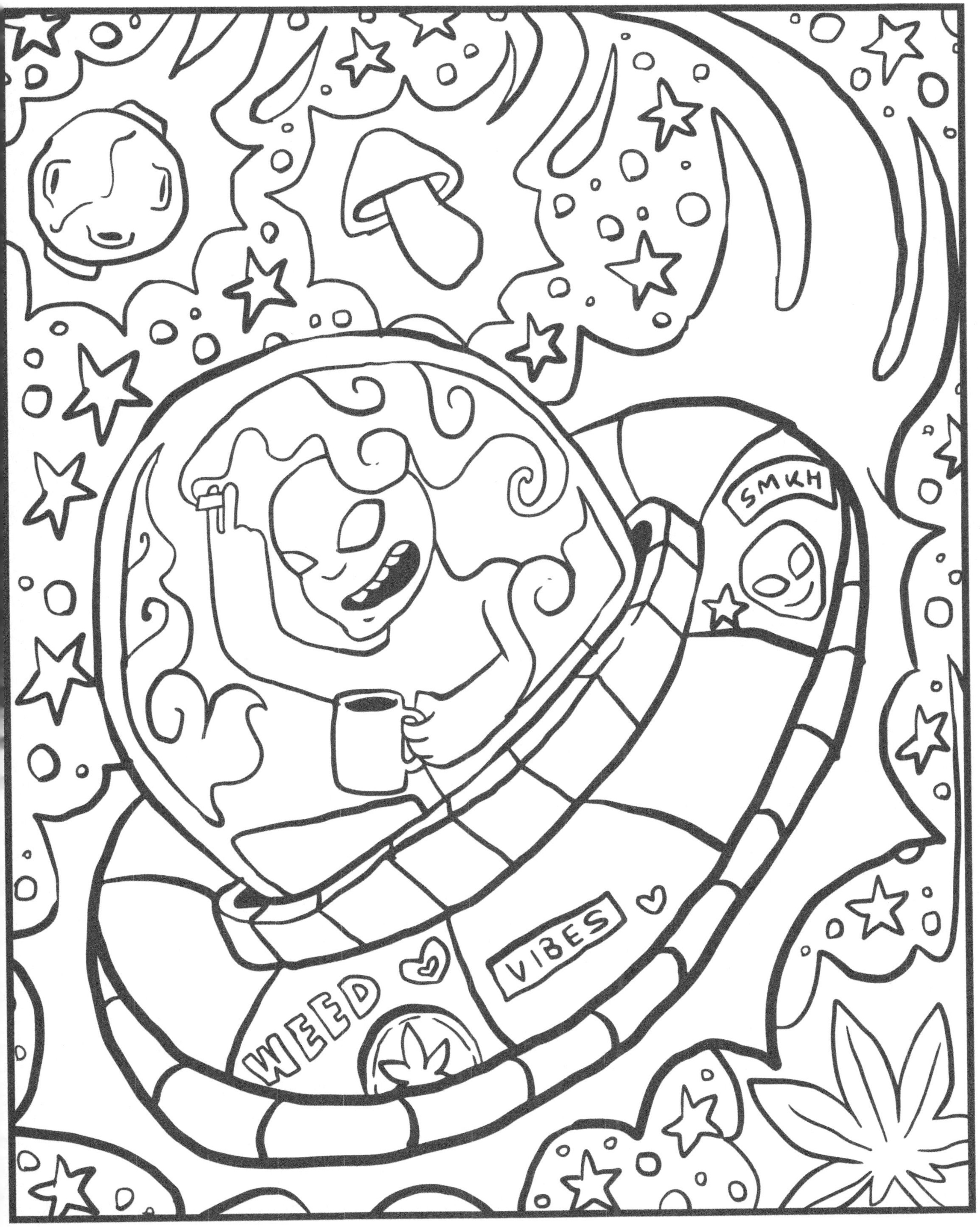
SMKH
VIBES
WEED

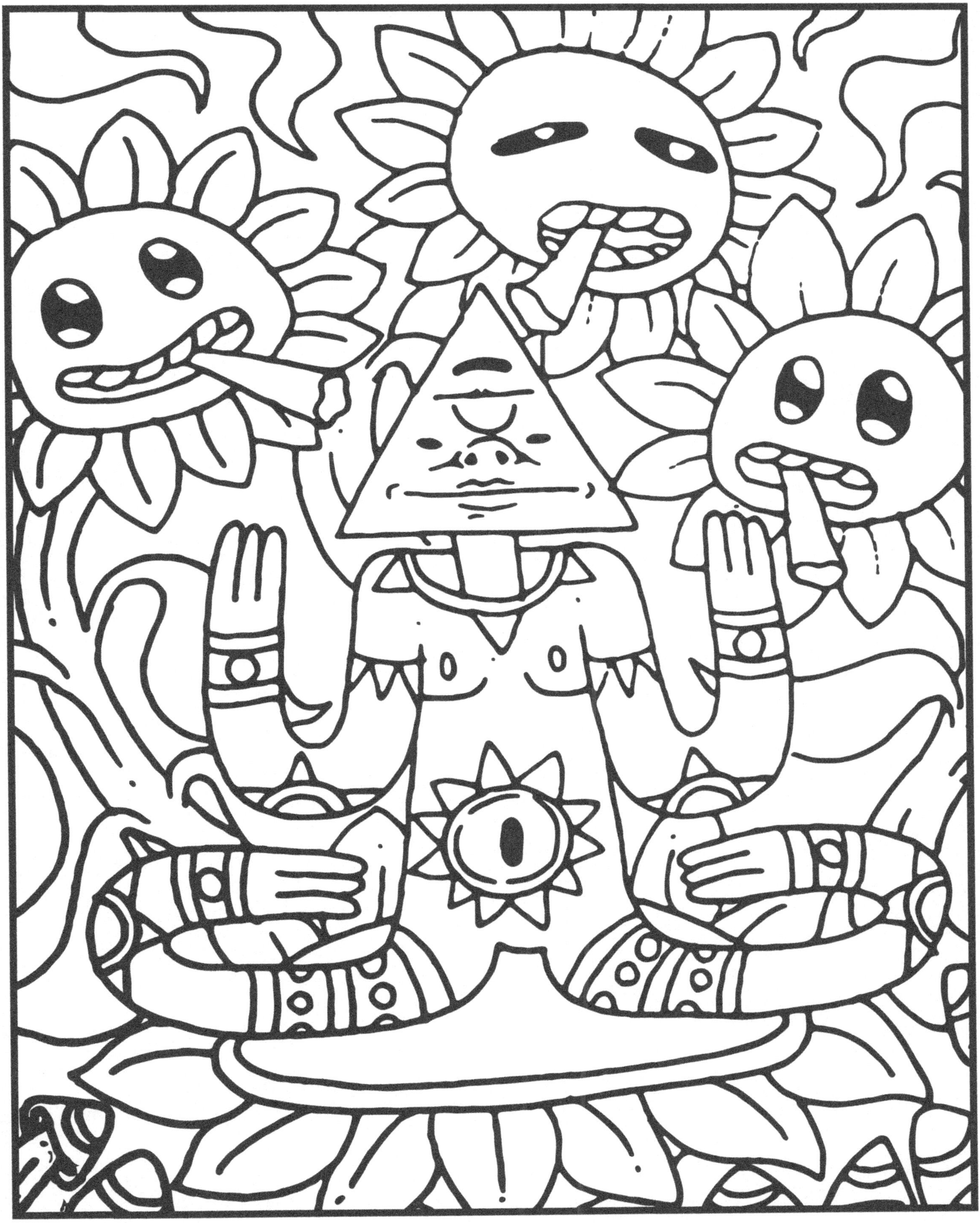

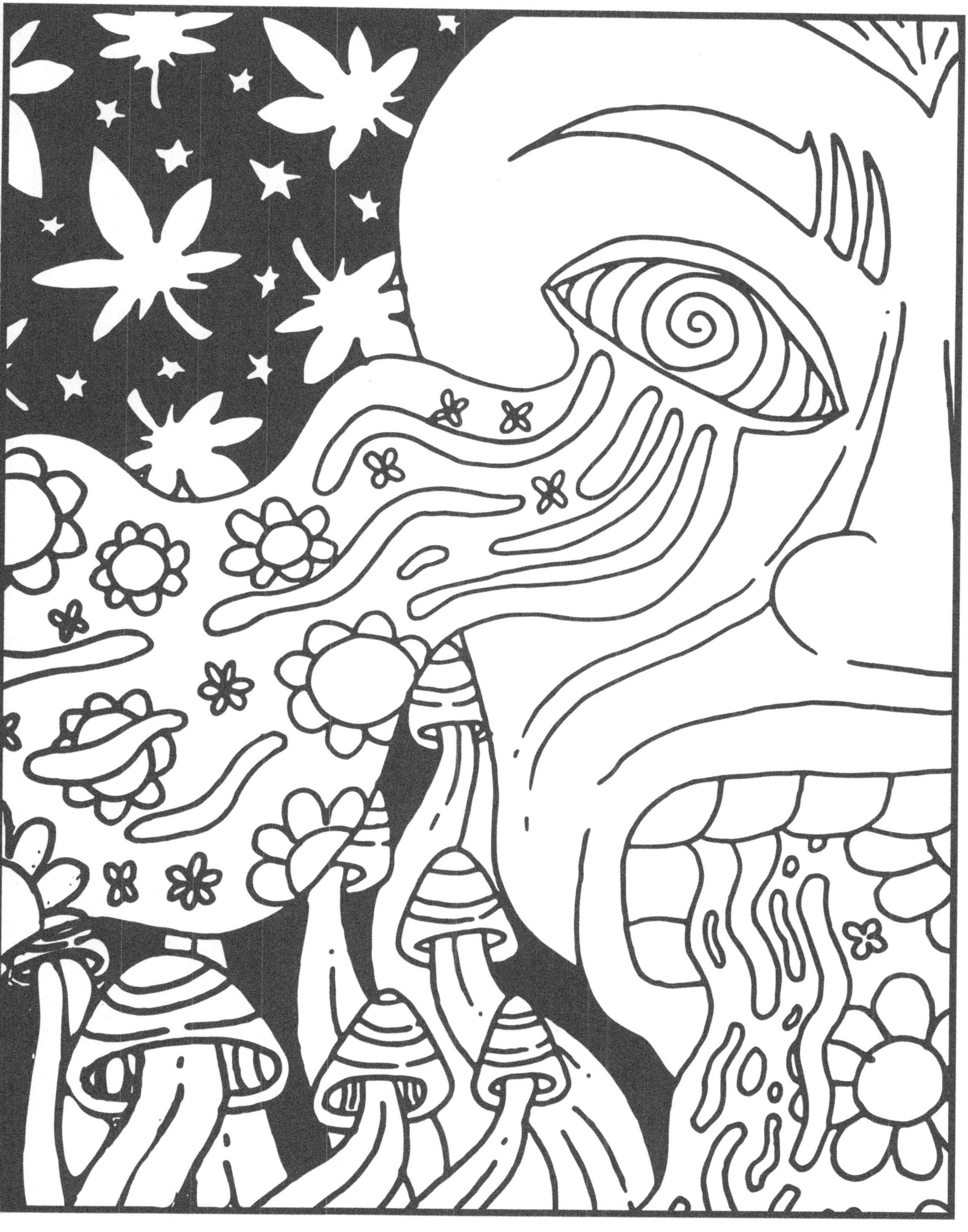

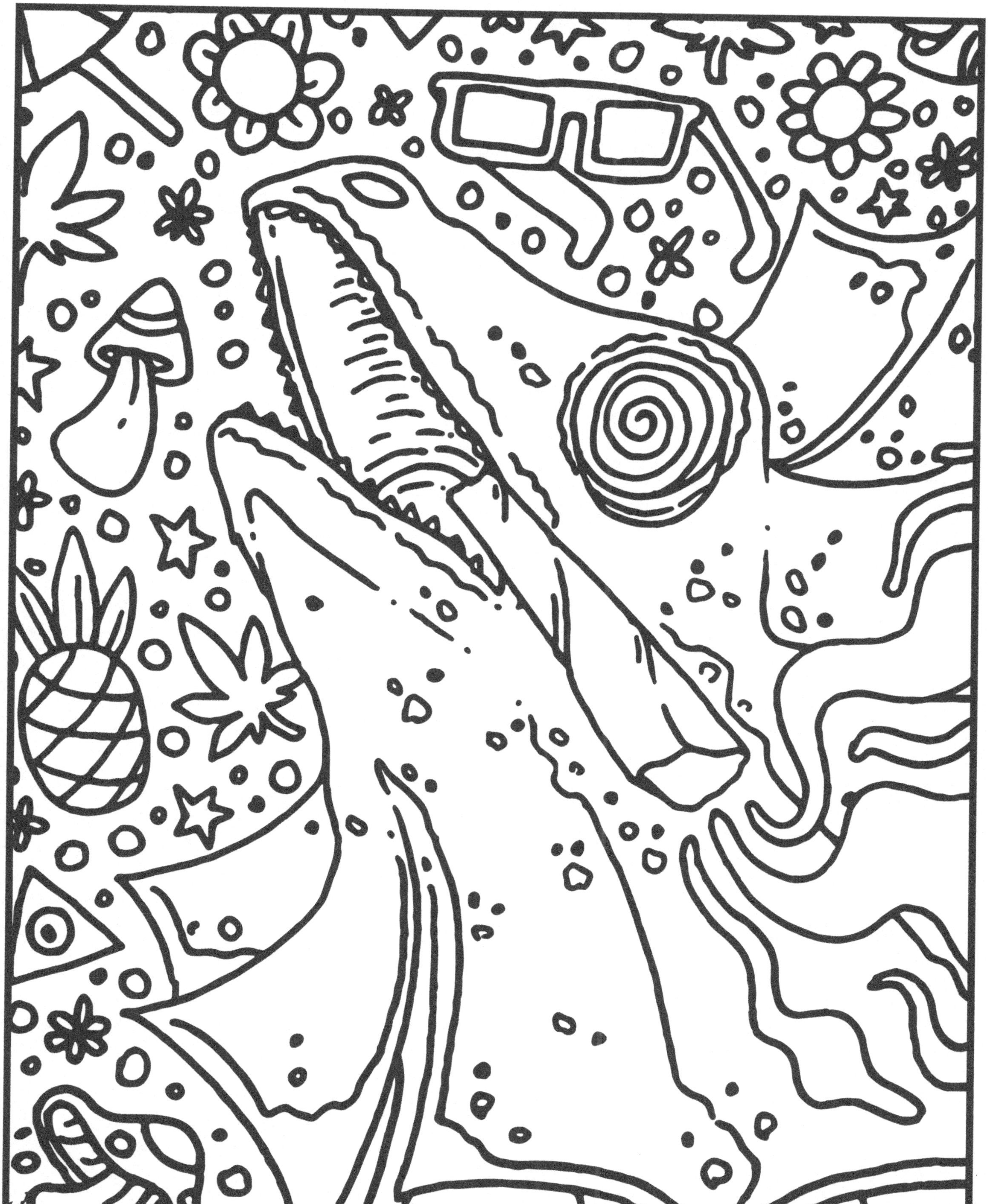

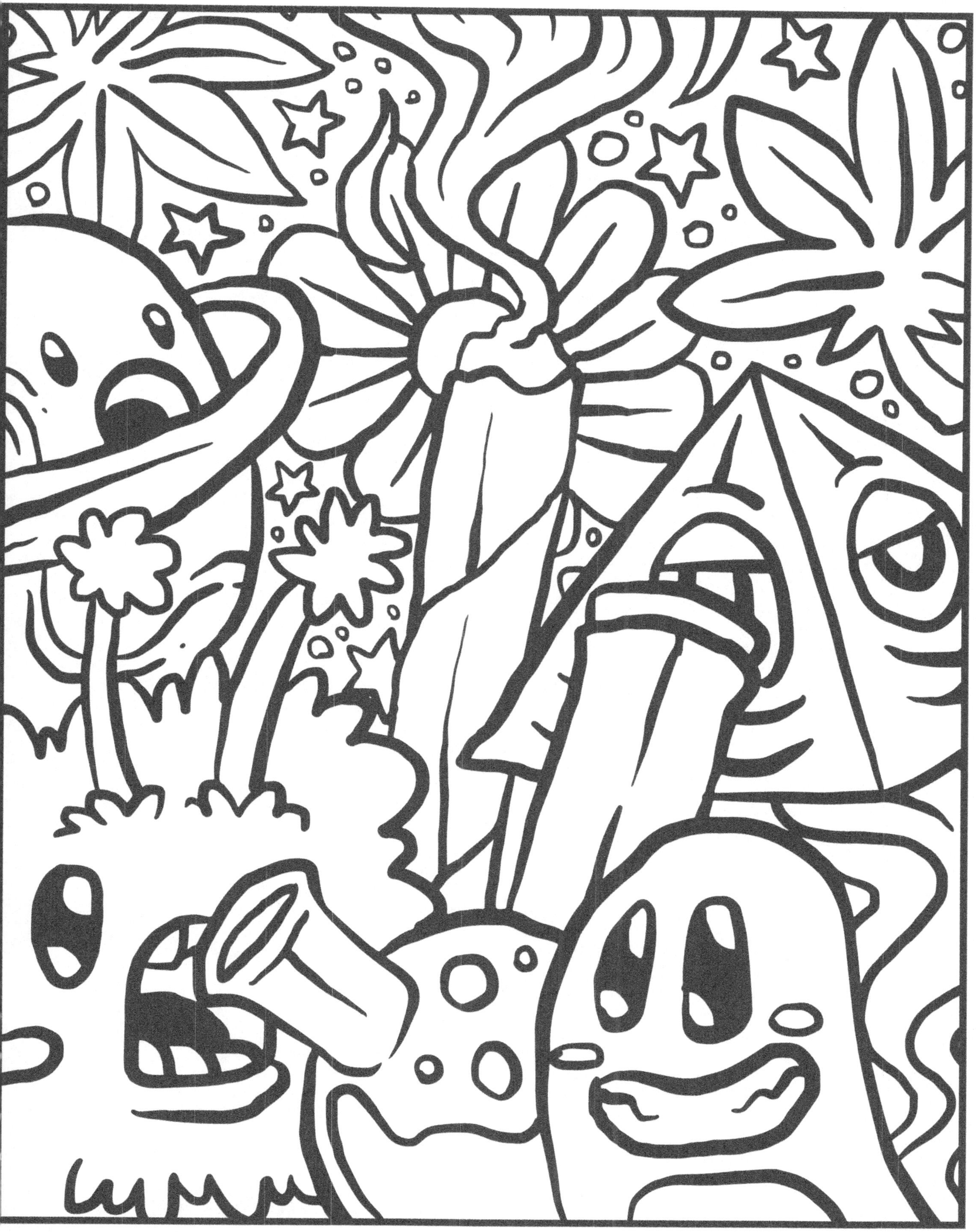

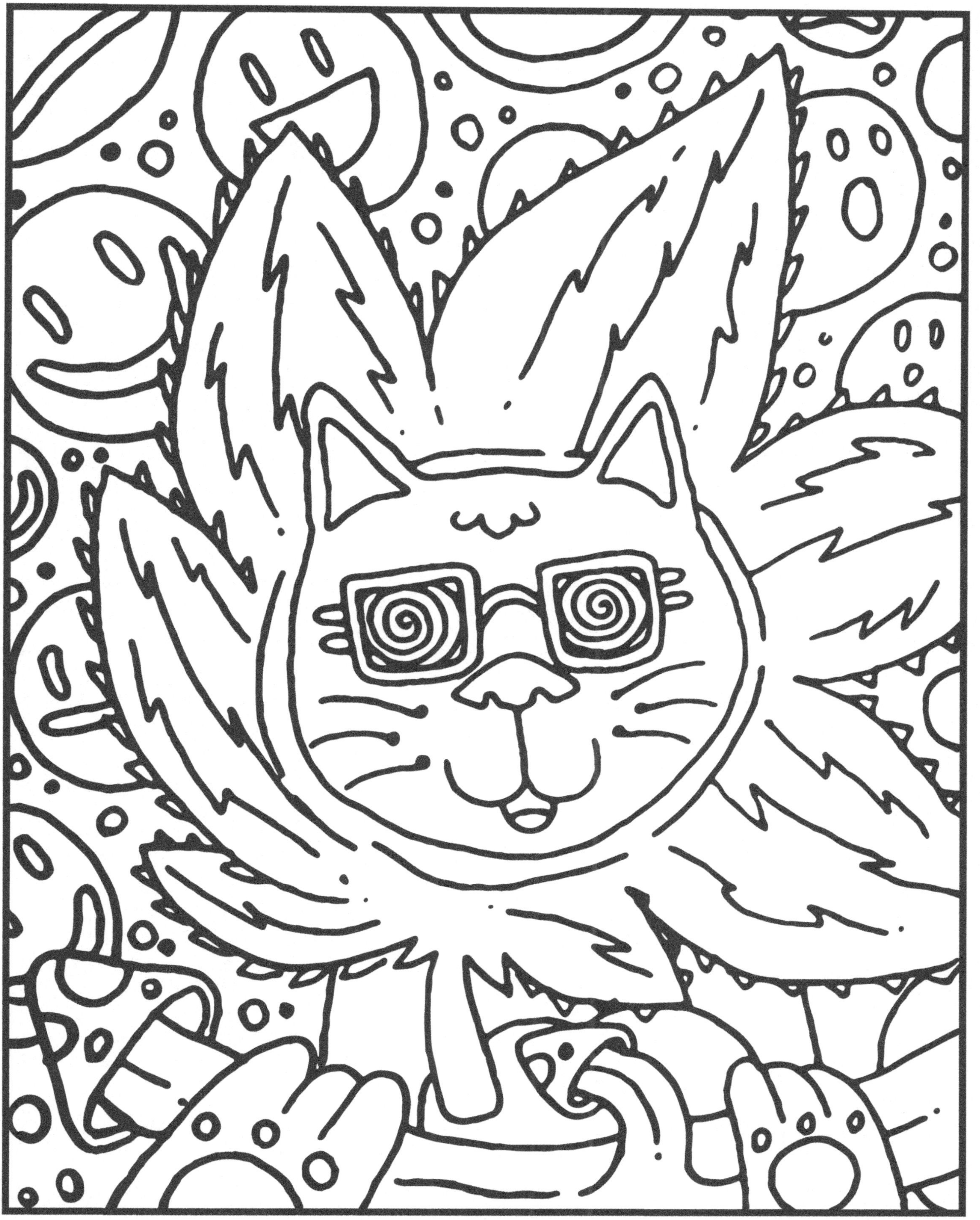

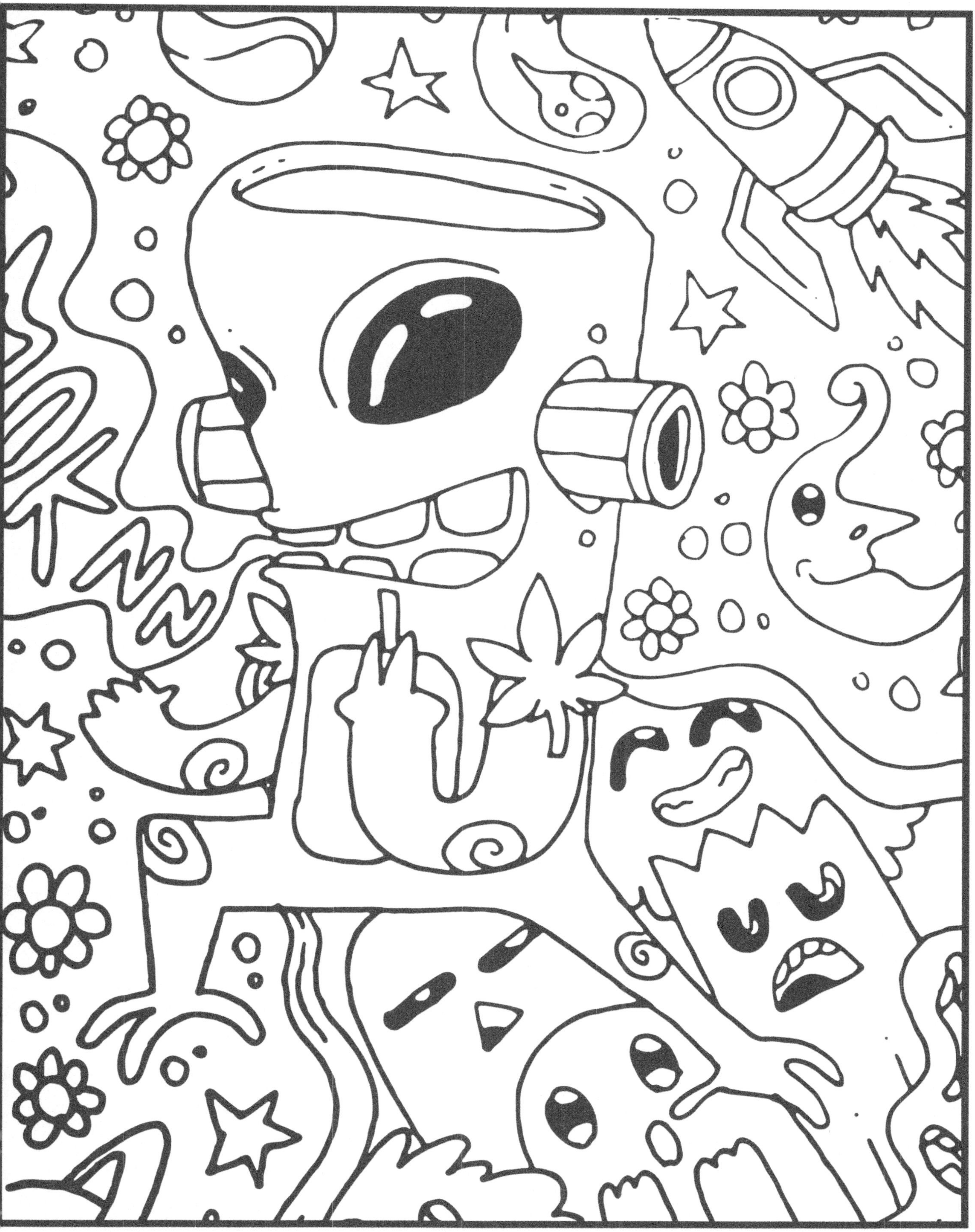

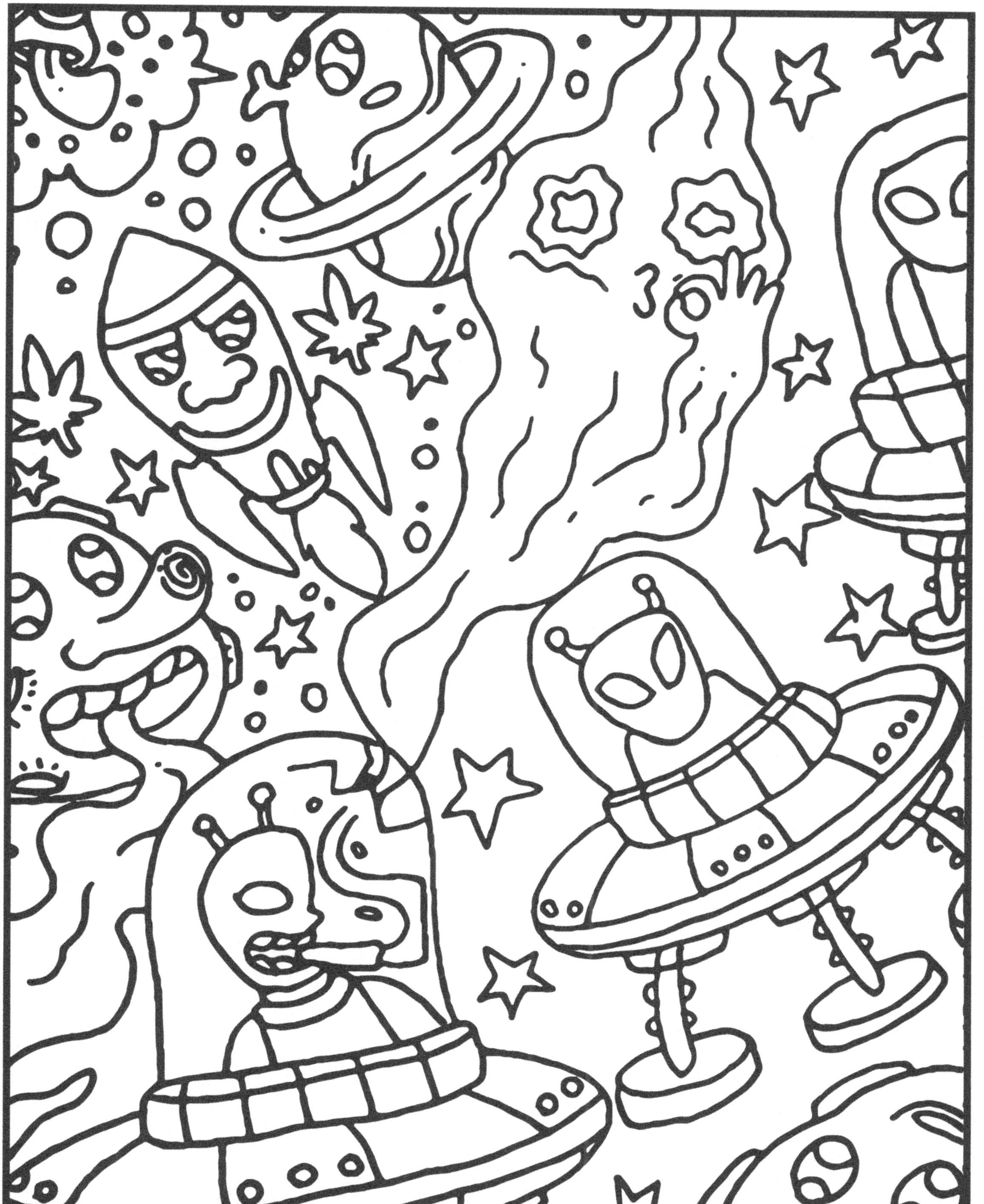

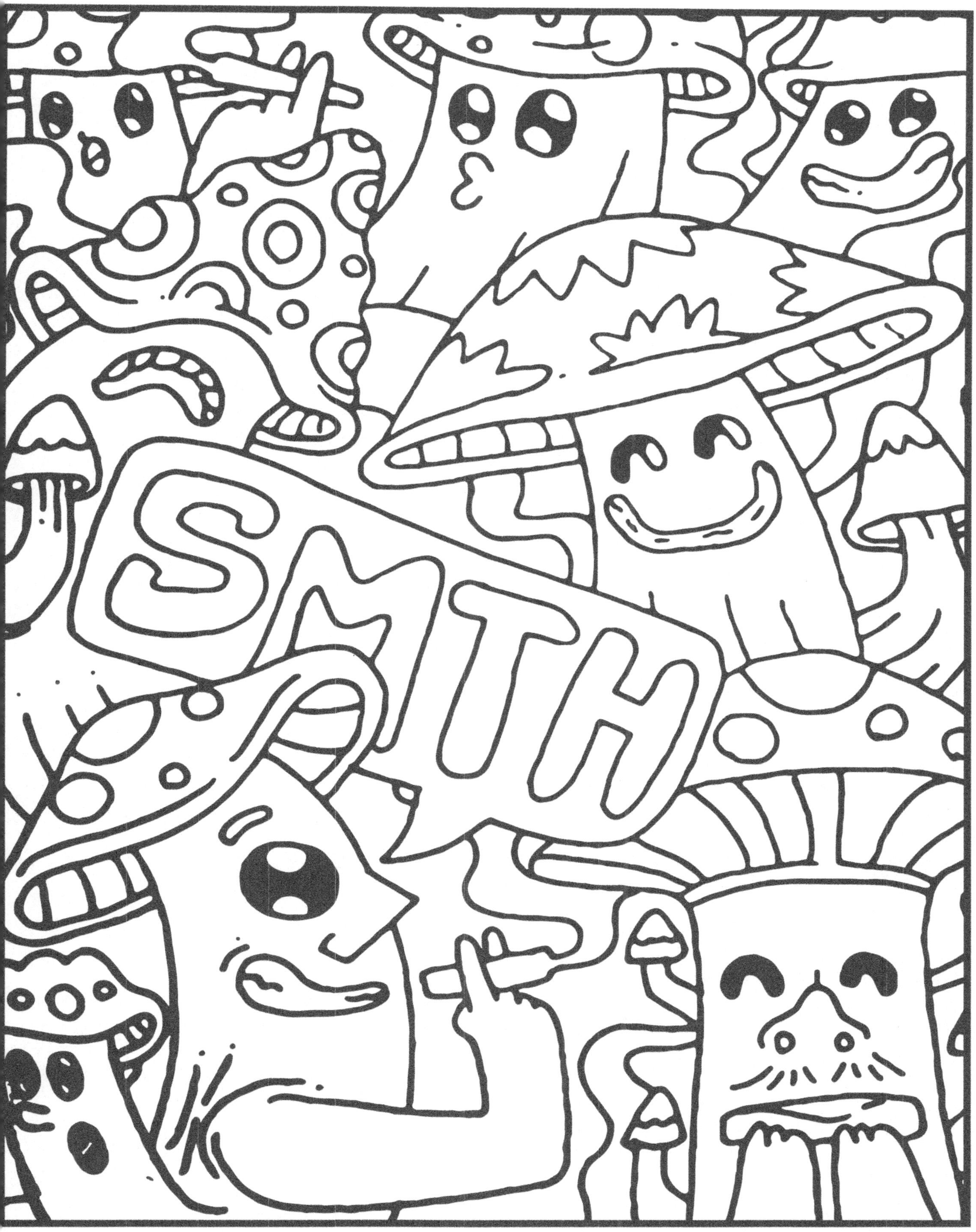
SMITH

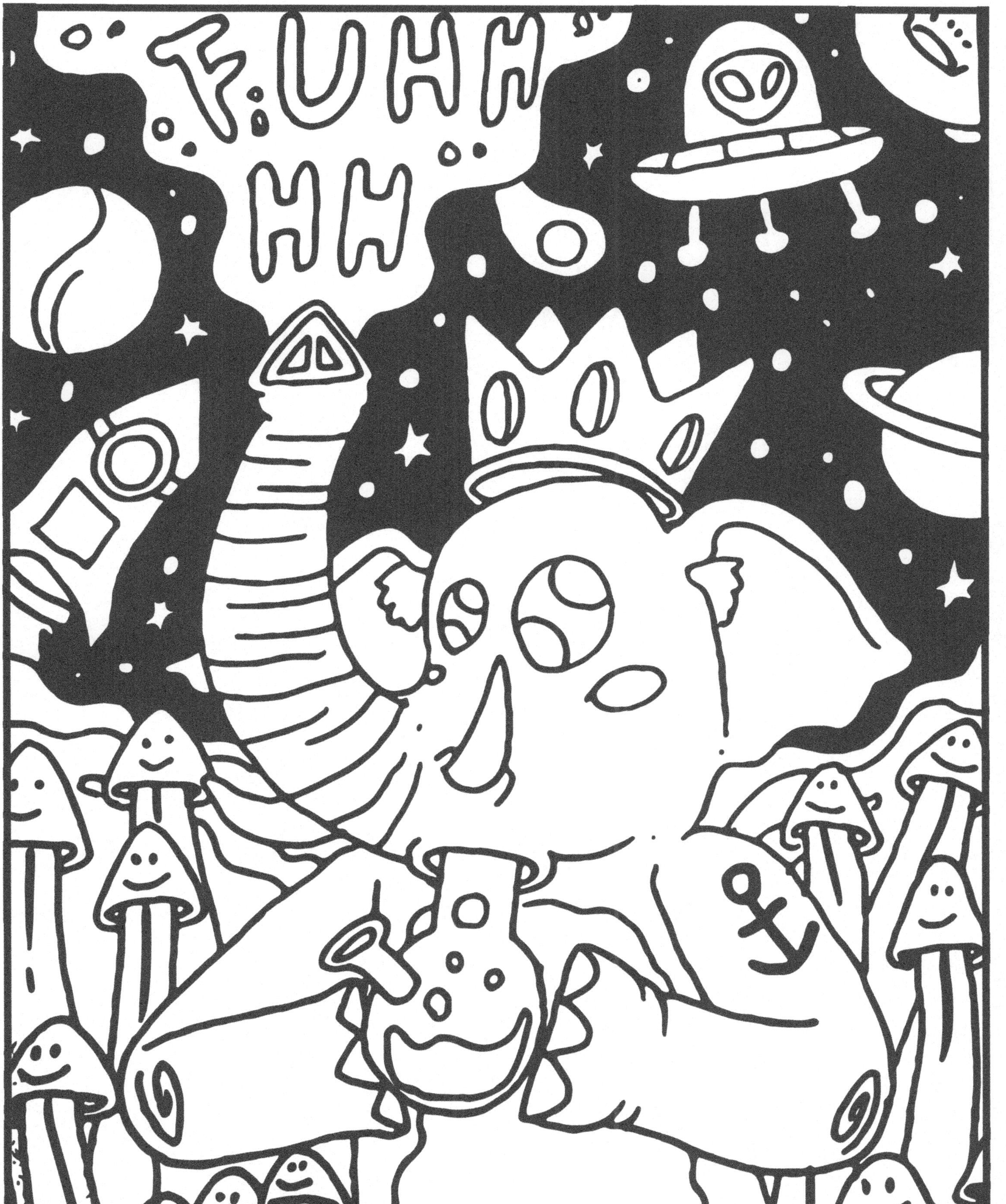
FUHH
HH

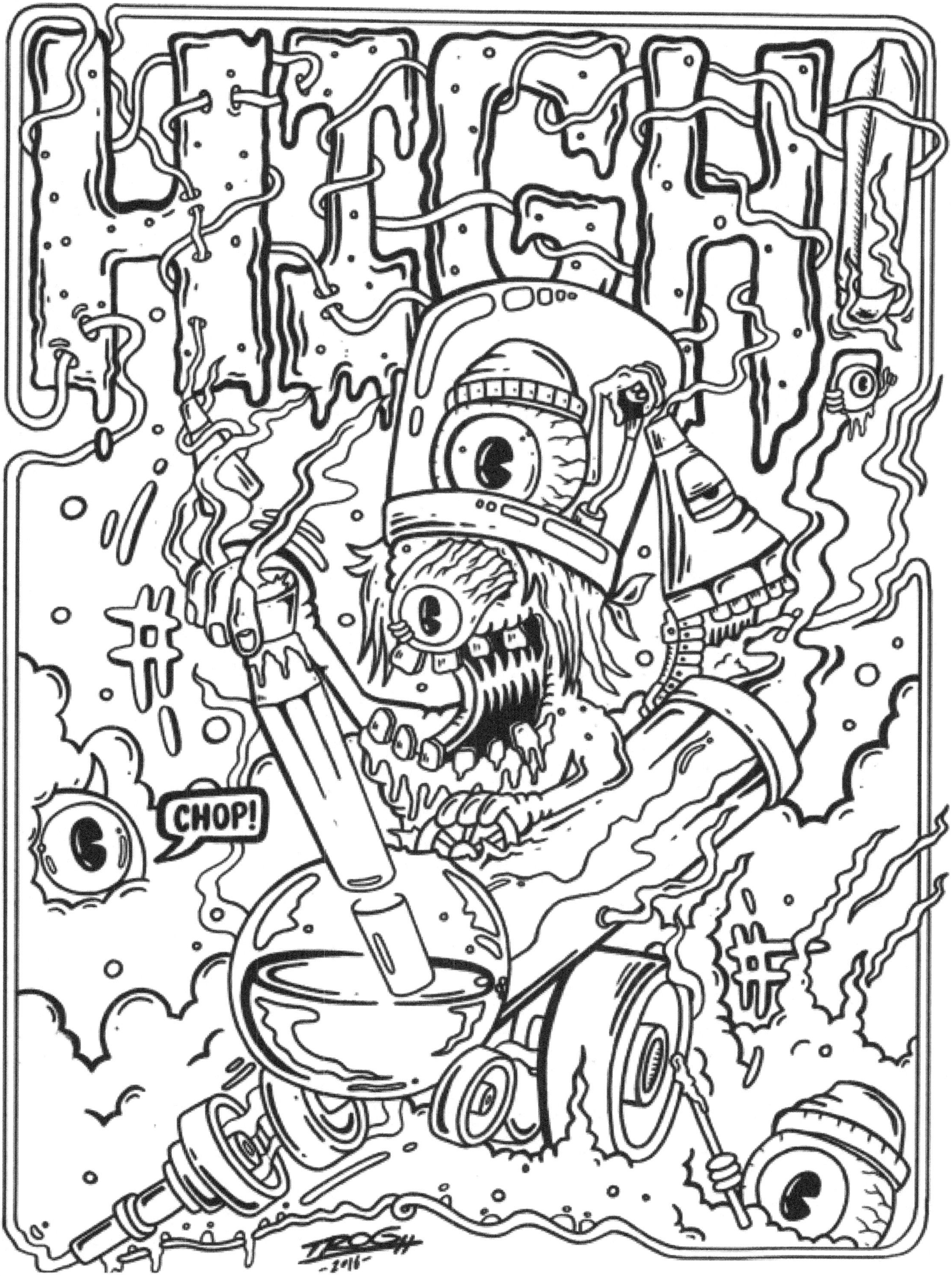
CHOP!

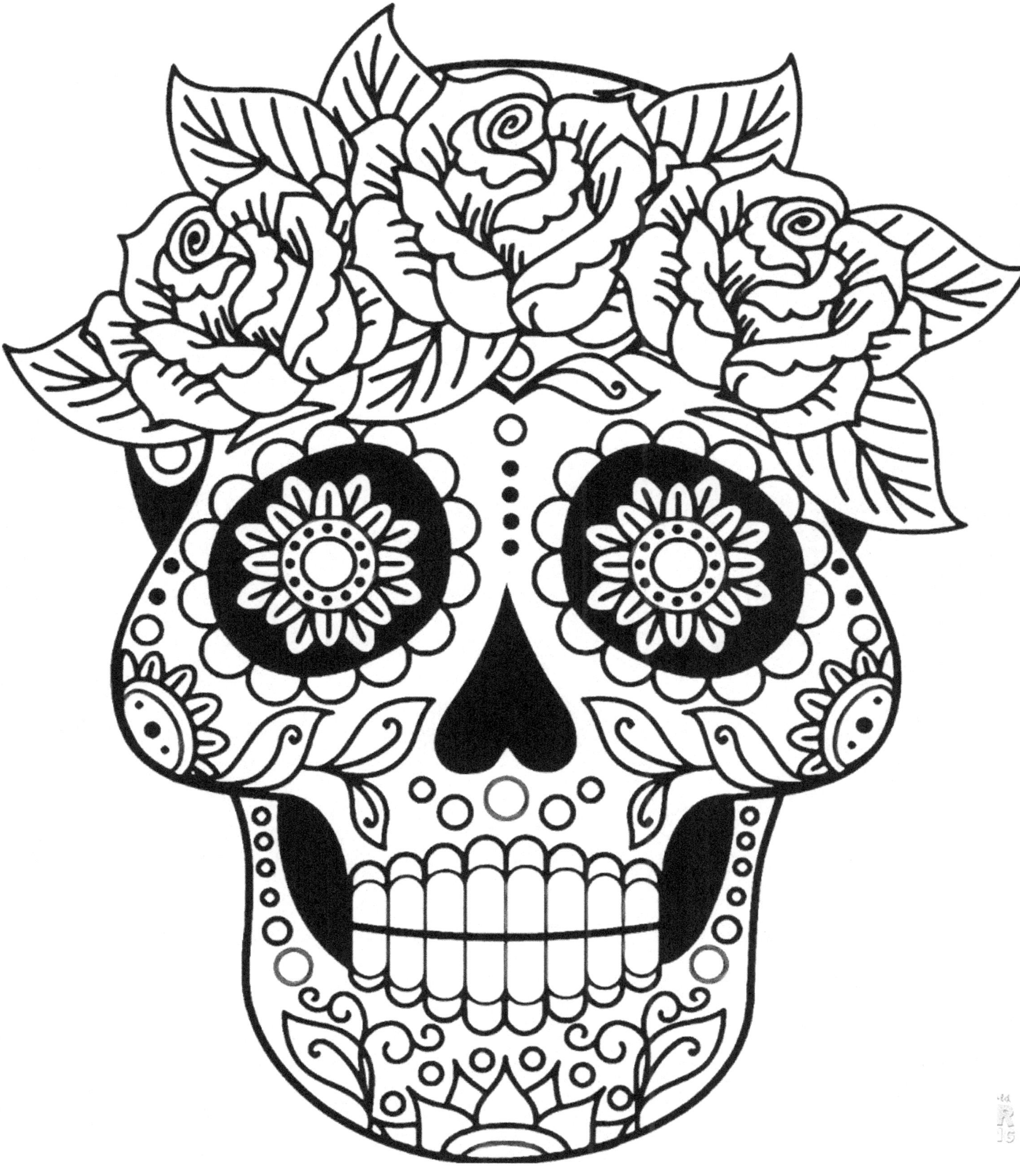

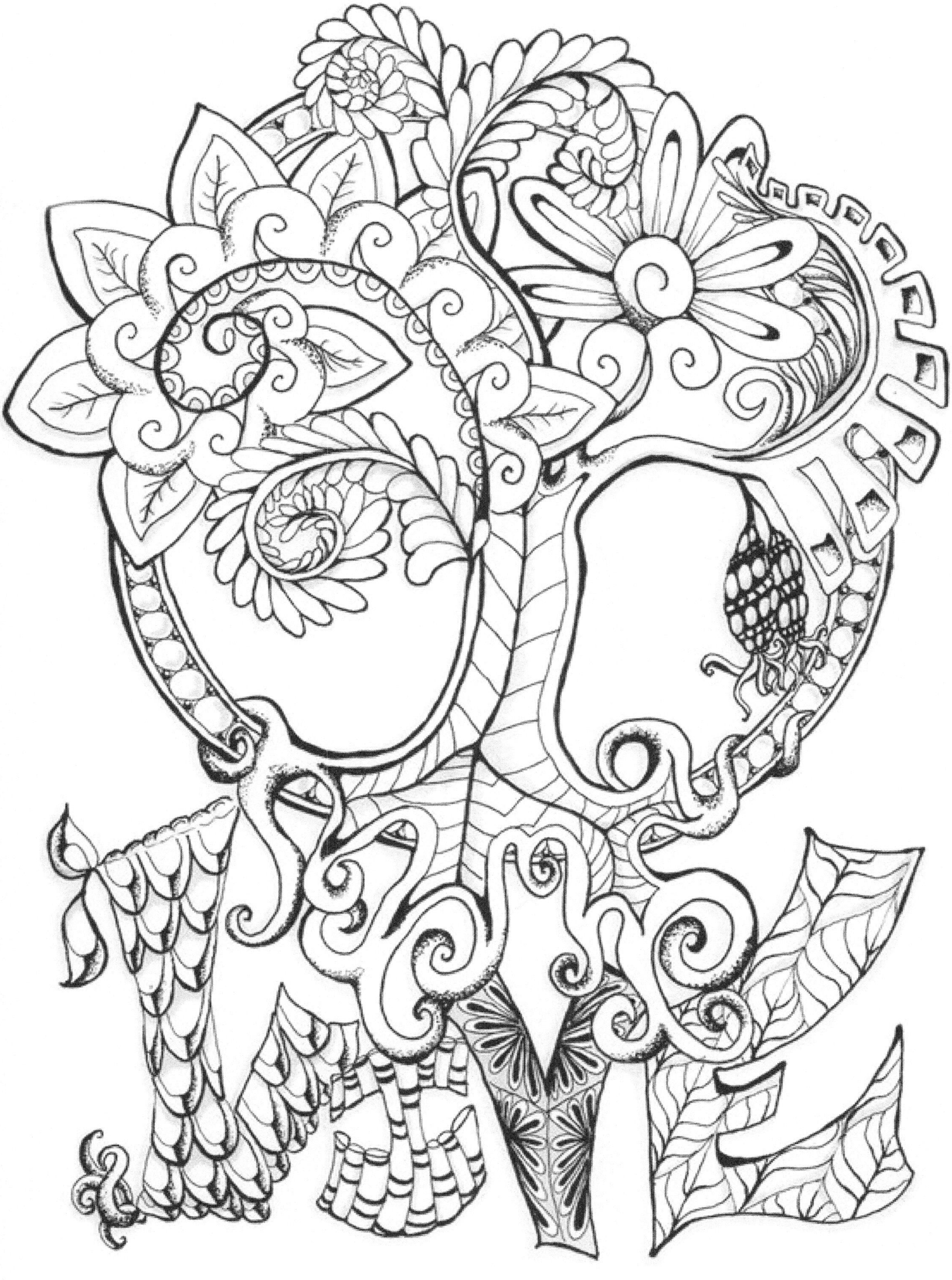

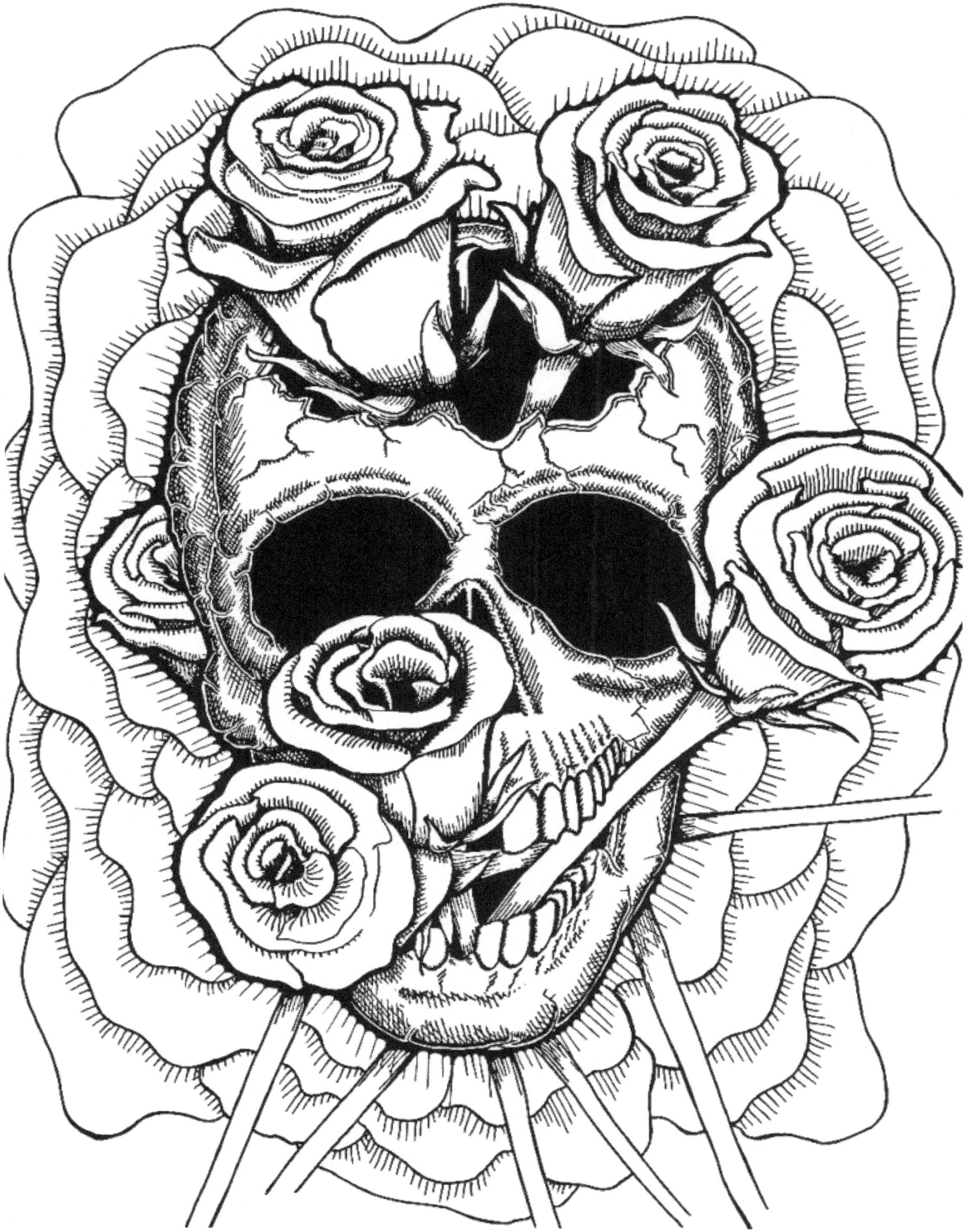

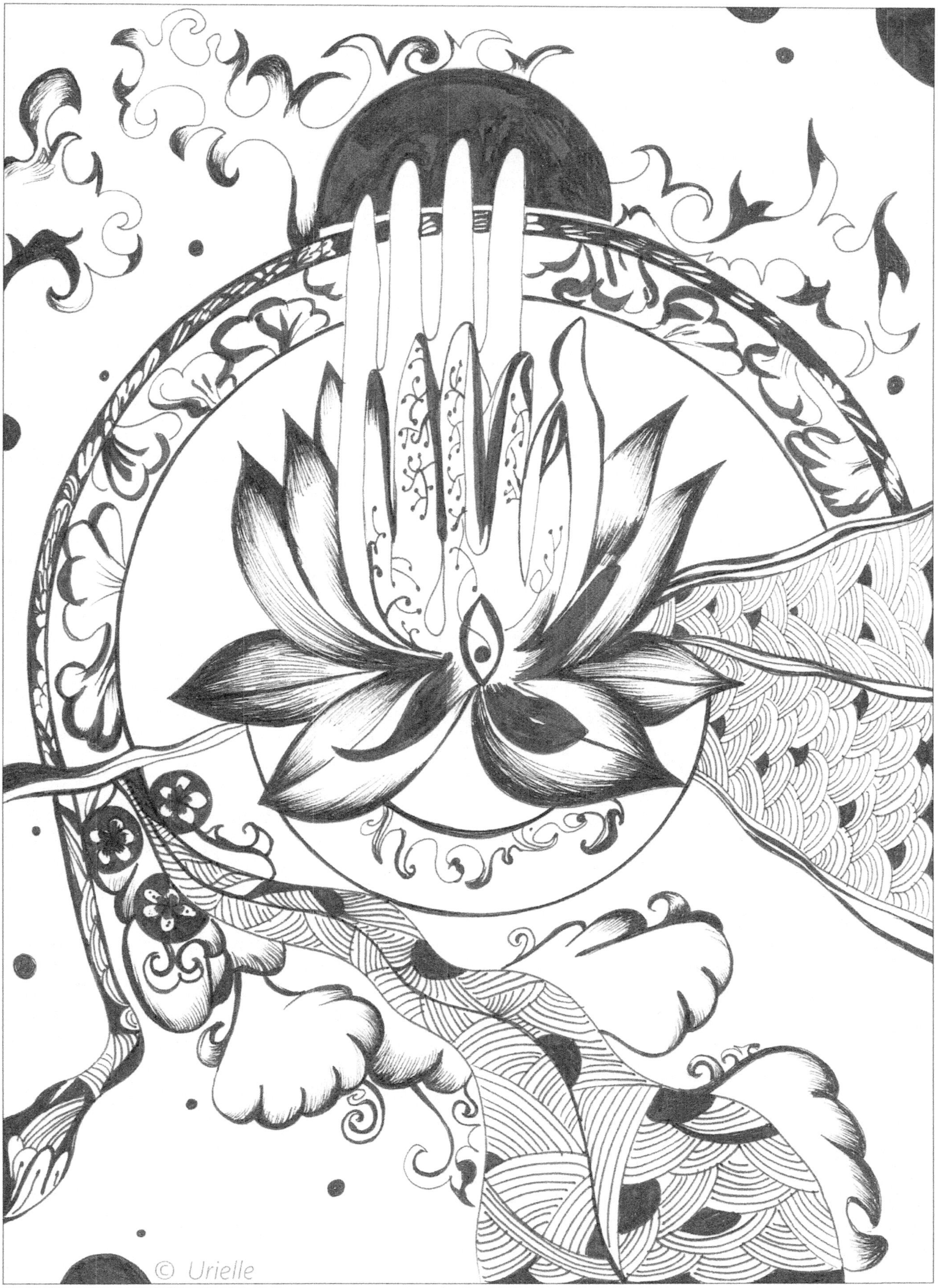
© Urielle

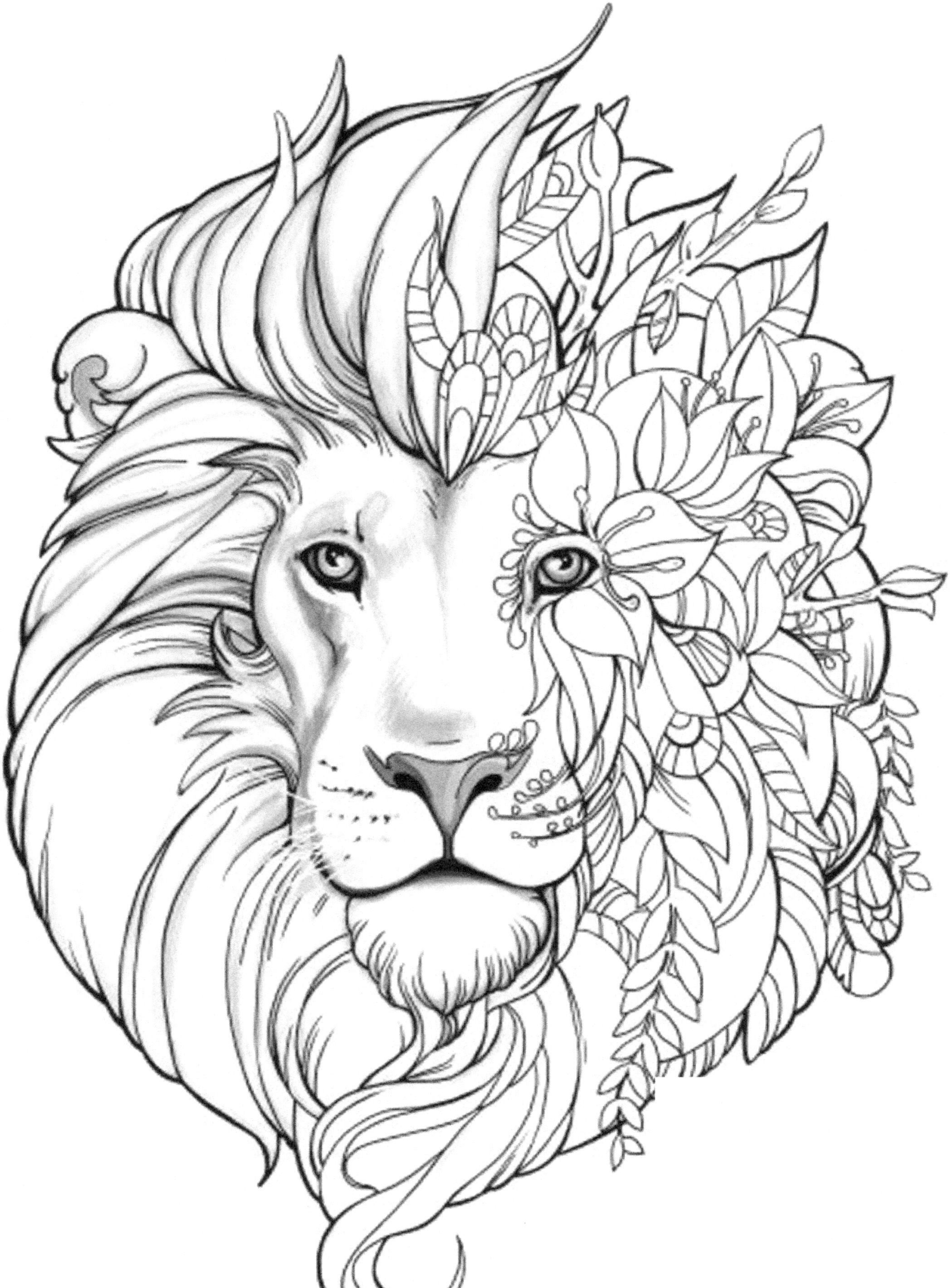

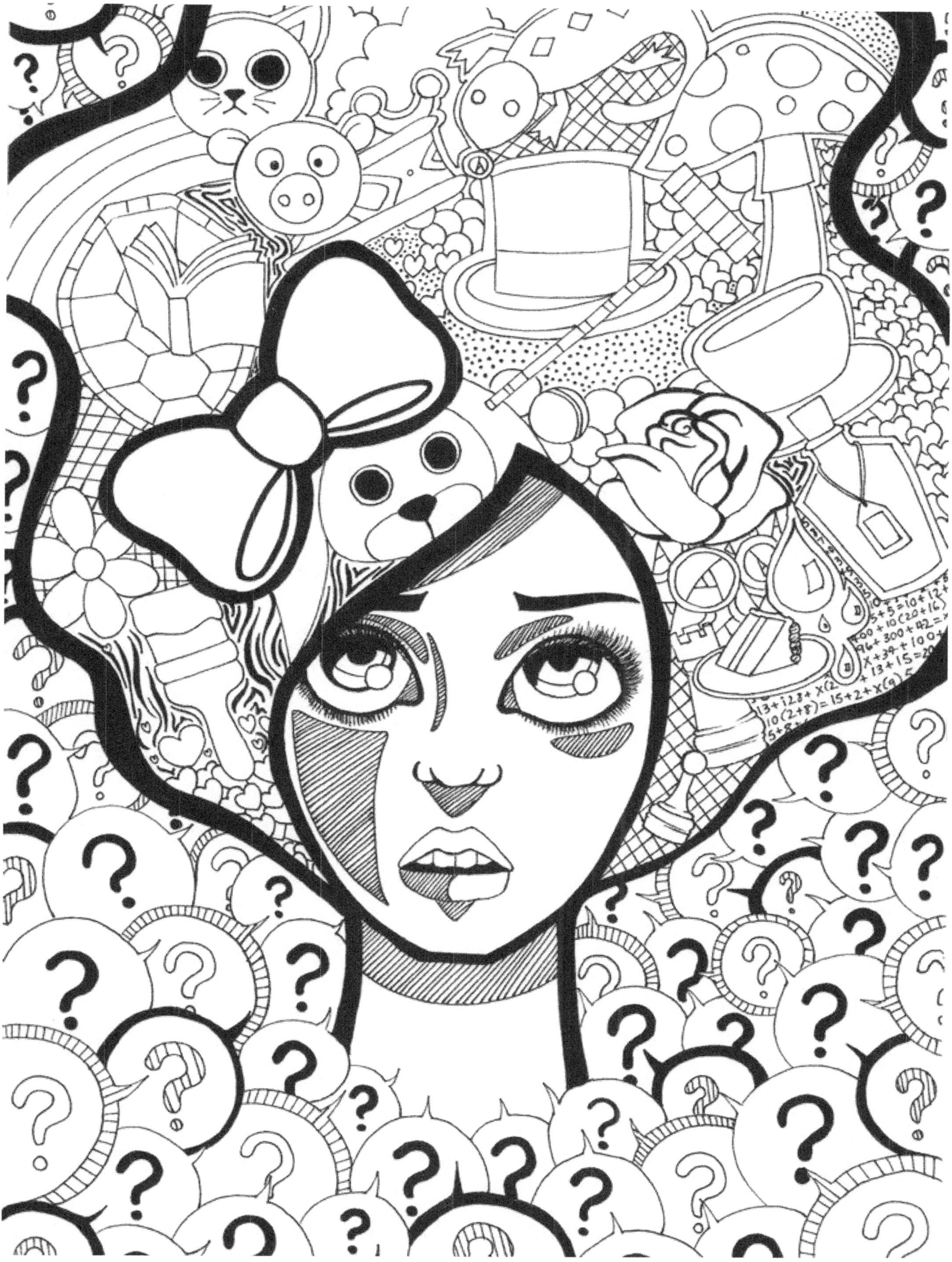

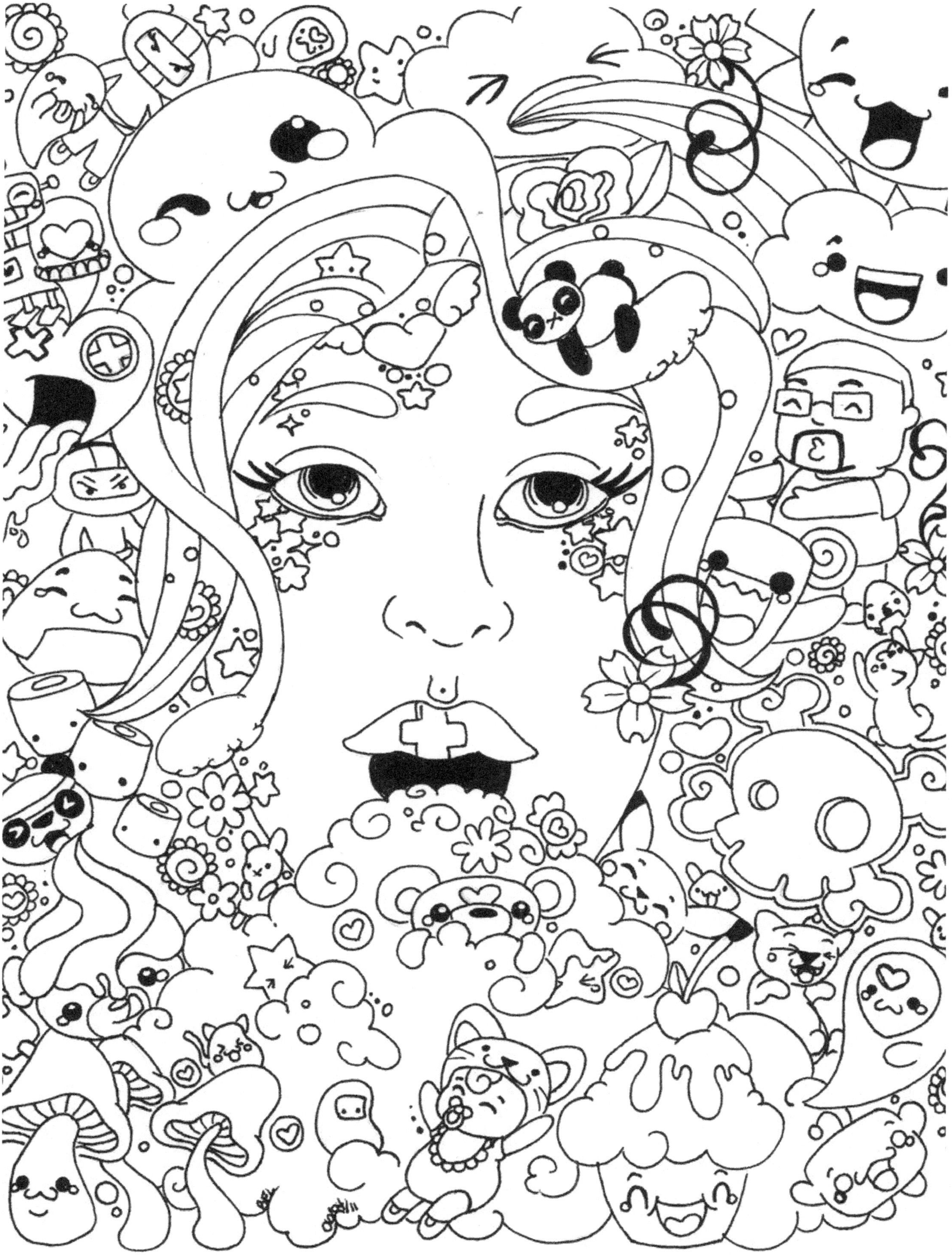

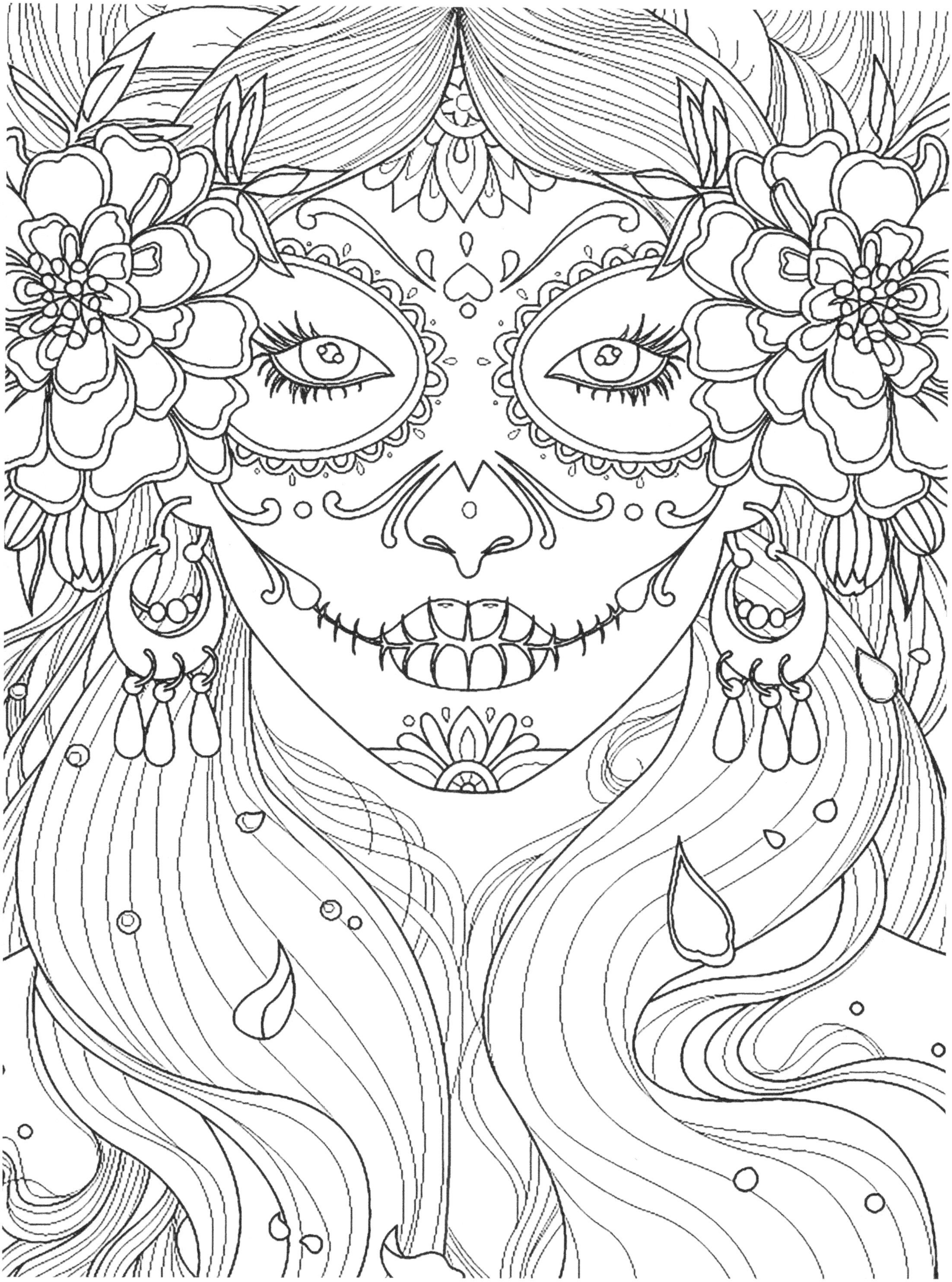

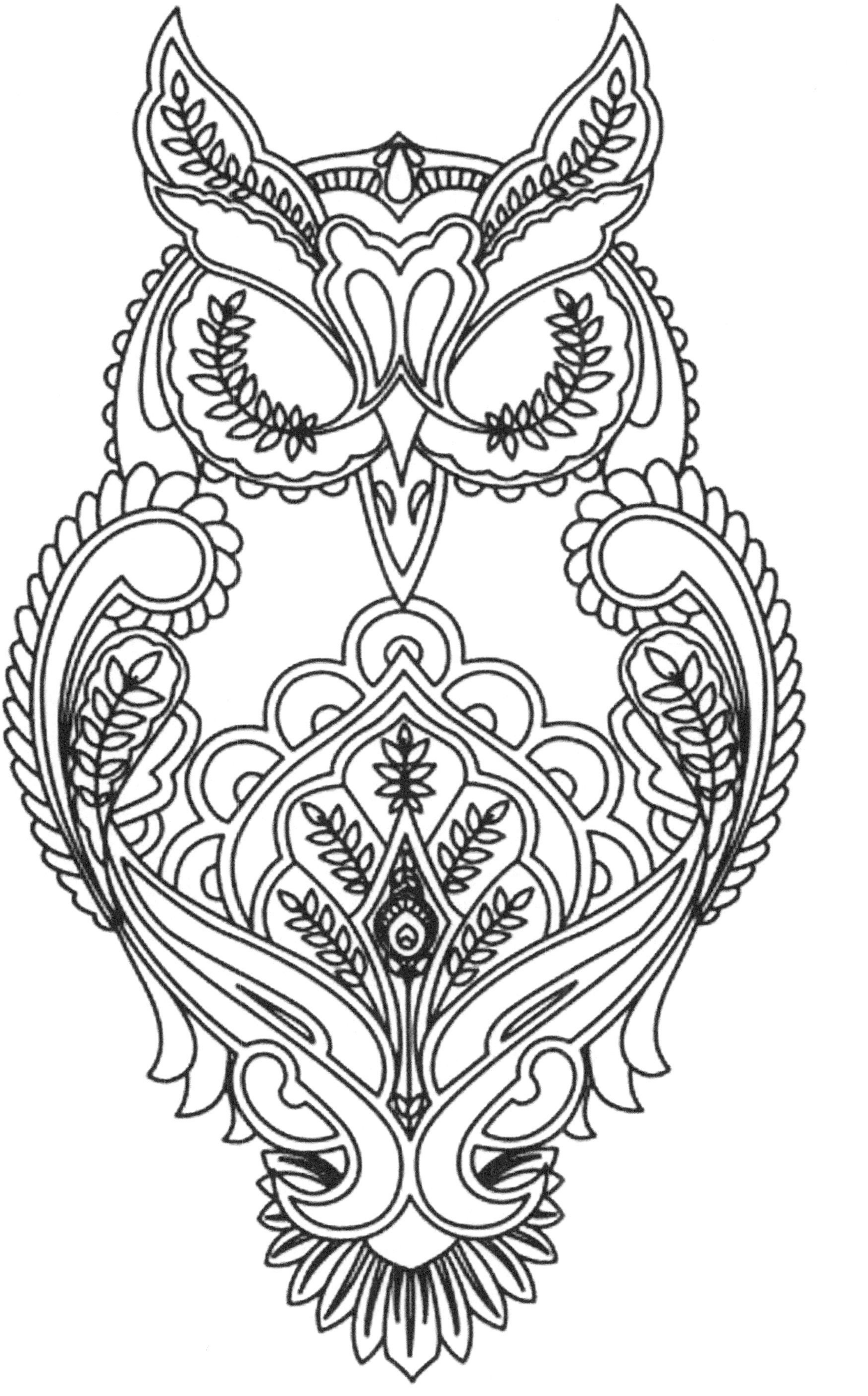

Made in the USA
Las Vegas, NV
27 July 2023

75322188R10039